Middle Eastern Cooking

*Eat together and do not eat separately,
for the blessing is with the company.*
Hadith, or saying of the Prophet Muhammad.

This edition first published in the United Kingdom 1994 by PRION,
an imprint of Multimedia Books Limited,
32-34 Gordon House Road, London NW5 1LP

Exclusive distribution in the USA by
Smithmark Publishers Inc.
16 East 32nd Street, New York, NY 10016

Managing Editor: Anne Johnson

Editor: Beverly LeBlanc

Production: Hugh Allan

Design: Kelly Flynn

Photography: Theo Bergström and Christine Osborne

ISBN 1 85375 146 4

Photoset by Northern Phototypesetting Co. Ltd., Bolton, Lancashire
Printed in Italy by Poligrafici Calderara SpA, Bologna, Italy

RIGHT *A woman baking bread*
in a traditional village oven in
Dhofar, southern Oman.

Middle Eastern Cooking

Christine Osborne

Contents

Foreword   6

Introduction   8

Mezze   20

Soups   42

Salads   54

Vegetables and Rice   66

Seafood   80

Meat   92

Poultry   110

Desserts and Confectioneries   124

Drinks   140

Index   150

Acknowledgments   152

TOP LEFT
Ripening dates in the Shatt el-Arab delta, southern Iraq.
TOP RIGHT
Boxed fruits from the West Bank of the river Jordan.
BOTTOM LEFT
Mezze as it is served in a Beirut restaurant.
BOTTOM RIGHT
Spices for sale in a spice market in downtown Amman.

A Bedouin pounding coffee beans in southern Jordan. Coffee is drunk at every opportunity throughout the Middle East.

6

Foreword

As you might imagine, I had many adventures in my endeavors to learn the secrets of Middle Eastern cooking.

Most unusual was a lunch in north Yemen in a restaurant no bigger than a large hole in the wall. This is precisely what it was, a cavity in the wall around the capital, Sana'a, into which an enterprising Yemeni had maneuvered some tables and chairs.

I had not finished eating when the space was invaded by crowds of men who, unable to squeeze past, walked across the top of my table. Then, finding a seat, they unclipped daggers and hung them on a hook as a westerner might his umbrella. No one paid me, the only woman, the slightest attention. As far as they knew, I might have been a *djinn!*

Quite the opposite was a lavish banquet in Saudi Arabia in honor of the visit of Her Majesty Queen Elizabeth II and the Duke of Edinburgh.

All that day refrigerated vans had sped the best of Arab and imported delicacies between Riyadh, the Saudi capital, and a spot in the desert, marked by a mammoth tent. Lobster had been flown in from Jeddah and truffles from France, and fifty lambs had been slaughtered for the occasion, which was to be attended by hundreds of sheikhs. The hospitable Saudis had even extended the invitation to the press – an unheard-of event in royal circles – which was how I found myself dining with the Queen, Her Majesty being obscured, however, by pyramids of dates.

Between these two remarkable occasions lie a wealth of memories and a host of meals – many of which are recaptured in *Middle Eastern Cooking.*

The current interest in Middle Eastern cooking is part of a western trend toward ethnic food. It also coincides with two significant events which, sadly, typify the Middle East in western minds.

The first is the agonizing civil war in Lebanon which has uprooted many thousands of Lebanese who have fled abroad and taken their cuisine with them. Many have subsequently opened restaurants, so today you can eat Middle Eastern food in almost any large city in the world.

The second event, more protracted, has been the nationalization of the Arab oil industry. Inestimable wealth disbursed by generous rulers now enables even the poorest Bedouin to enjoy a vacation abroad. The first Arab tourists took cooks with them to prepare meals according to Muslim dietary laws, and it was not long before leading hotels in London and Paris were employing Muslim chefs, exposing westerners to Middle Eastern cuisine.

The taste of Middle Eastern food was brought to Britain, where I live, by business travelers and tour groups returning from trips. Expatriates employed in places such as Iraq and Iran also enthused about the local cooking.

Consequently, there is an enormous curiosity about Middle Eastern cooking, but most restaurants serve only a limited number of dishes. This does not mean that *Middle Eastern Cooking* will unveil a thousand and one recipes; what it will do is pass on a few of the most popular, so that anyone with a working knowledge of cooking can make them.

Other recipes are missing for obvious reasons. It is not feasible to try smoking Iraqi *mashgouf* around a fire in your kitchen. Nor is it feasible to cook *khouzi*, an Arab dish requiring a whole sheep. Without help, confections such as *knaffeh* and Turkish Delight are very time-consuming to prepare. Today's Middle Eastern housewife usually buys them ready-made.

Bread is also frequently purchased from the baker, who makes several batches throughout the day. Many loaves are too big to bake in a domestic oven and are cooked in a large, beehive-shaped oven, or *tanour*. Similar types are sold in Lebanese and Turkish food stores or, failing this, the Greek pita and Indian naan are similar. On a recent visit to Sydney, I discovered *khoubz* in a supermarket.

As an Australian, I was brought up on beef, but since leaving Sydney in 1963, I have traveled extensively in the Muslim world, where beef is uncommon. By now I have visited every country in the Middle East – and north Africa for good measure.

My interest in local food developed after an initial visit to Beirut, the focal point of Middle Eastern cooking. Like any western visitor, I was eager to acquire some recipes to entertain at home. I did not want anything too elaborate, because, like most working women, cooking time is limited to weekends, but I sought some easily prepared dishes for entertaining on busy weeknights.

I trust the same applies to you, and that *Middle Eastern Cooking* will bring new pleasures to your table. *Bismillah!**

CHRISTINE OSBORNE

**Bismillah! (in the name of God!),*
as expressed by an Arab before eating.

Introduction

Media coverage of the seventeen-year civil war in Lebanon, and the more recent Gulf War, gives the impression that the Middle East is a land of blazing guns. Yet, the millions of citizens going to work in Cairo or Ankara, or the *felaheen* toiling in the fields, represent a far more accurate picture of daily life.

The belly of the Orient, the Middle East sweeps east from Egypt through the countries of the Fertile Crescent as far as Iran and encompasses the vast land mass of the Arabian peninsula. The majority of people speak Arabic and share a common heritage, with colorful regional variations in music, costume and cuisine.

While parts of the Middle East are largely desert, elsewhere is lush and green, as the name the Fertile Crescent implies. Other areas are even subtropical, like the beautiful palm-fringed coast of Dhofar in southern Oman. Between these extremes is a rugged mix of pebble plains and dunes where Bedouin nomads still migrate from oasis to oasis.

According to archaeologists and historians, civilization in the Middle East began sometime in the fifth century B.C. in Mesopotamia.

We know little about the diet of the ancient peoples, but it seems likely that they had the same pulse-based dishes as the *felaheen* of today, and because the region was rich in wildlife, game birds, gazelle and wild boar were probably popular.

Ancient civilizations and conquering armies have bequeathed to the Middle East a rich architectural heritage: the remains of giant dams, soaring pyramids, and magical-sounding cities such as Persepolis and Petra. In the absence of records, we can only assume that people with such building expertise also possessed sophisticated culinary skills.

The expansion of the Greek and Roman empires undoubtedly contributed to the cuisine in the Middle East, and the spread of Islam from Arabia introduced humble but wholesome foods.

Ruling from Baghdad, the Abbasid dynasty (A.D. 750–1258) is known to have been passionately interested in cooking. Many popular present-day recipes have origins in Abbasid kitchens.

The Ottoman Empire introduced the stuffed vegetable dishes so popular in Middle Eastern cooking. British and French mandates following the World War I also added new ideas, but by then Middle Eastern cooking styles were firmly established, and while western dishes were applauded, local habits remained unchanged.

The amalgam of so many cuisines makes Middle Eastern food unique and at the same time difficult to define. Basically it can be described as wholesome and well flavored, spicy without being fiery hot, and notable for several items in particular: *mezze* or appetizers, stuffed vegetables and meats, and rich confectioneries. It is not merely the food, however, that ranks Middle Eastern cooking – none too soon – with the world's greatest cuisines, but its presentation and the surroundings in which it is served.

REGIONAL COOKING – THE LEVANT

While Middle Eastern cooking follows a basic theme, there are regional variations: Levantines eat more grilled meat and yogurt than, say, the Yemenis; Yemenis, on the other hand, like spicy dishes; Persian recipes dabble in a subtle combination of fruit and meat; curries have crept into the Arab cuisine, and so on. There is little difference in etiquette except where contact with the West has influenced customs.

The countries of the eastern Mediterranean littoral, or the Levant – Lebanon, Syria and Jordan – enjoy a similar cuisine; however, the same dish may be called by different names, which is rather confusing, in the same way that cooking methods – a pinch of this or a handful of that – are often vague. Of the three cuisines, Jordanian cooking is most basic, a mix of Bedouin food from the eastern desert and warming dishes from the western escarpment. Syrian cooking tends to be more elaborate, while the best known, Lebanese, is noted for the stylish presentation of food and the infinite variety of dishes.

The flavors of Lebanon are those most commonly associated with Middle Eastern cooking: the tangy taste of chopped mint, garlic and lemon juice in an olive oil dressing; the smoky taste of purées made from roasted sesame seeds and grilled eggplants; the subtle taste of rose water in desserts. While the aroma of Turkish coffee percolates the entire Middle East, this too is unmistakably Lebanese.

If any race lives to eat, it is the affable Lebanese; a nation of shrewd entrepreneurs who find any excuse a good reason to mix business with the pleasure of eating. In Arabic, the word *lebnan* is derived from an Aramaic word meaning white, a reference to the snow-covered mountains behind Beirut but also to *laban*, which in

LEFT *Scales fly off a fine bream in Muscat, Sultanate of Oman. The Omanis are great fish-eaters.* RIGHT *A farmer's wife sifting through pulses before making a soup in Upper Egypt.*

LEFT *A Bedouin woman making buttermilk the traditional way in Dubai. She will sit and shake the liquid all day.*
RIGHT *In from the country, an old man shopping in a Jerusalem souk.*

Lebanon means curdled milk, a dish of thick, creamy yogurt being a popular *mezze*.

Mezze, or appetizers, are the best-known aspect of Lebanese cuisine. They consist of many small dishes, either true *hors d'oeuvres* or miniature main courses, spread out for people to serve themselves as in a Scandinavian *smörgasbord*. Some of the endless *mezze* recipes are described in the first chapter.

A typical meal may consist solely of *mezze* or have several courses, such as stuffed meat and vegetable dishes, *kebabs*, a fish or poultry dish, salads and rice, ending with fresh fruit, confectioneries and coffee. A water pipe, or *nargila*, may be brought in for the men, its gentle bubbling adding to the convivial atmosphere. *Arak* is commonly drunk with *mezze*. Lebanon also produces some of the best wines in the Middle East. The Lebanese particularly like eating out-of-doors, it being debatable whether they or the Turks invented the custom of *al fresco* dining.

Syrian food is equally appetizing, with a fondness for *mezze* shared with the Lebanese. *Bulghur* is widely used in cooking, and Syrian housewives are reputedly the best *kibbeh* makers in the Middle East. Seafood is available on the Mediterranean coast.

Part of the Fertile Crescent, Syria is self-sufficient in vegetables and fruit – pears, grapes and delicious figs. Preserved apricots are a specialty of Damascus. Together with almonds and walnuts, pistachio nuts are used in the desserts and confectioneries at which Syrian pastry bakers excel. Aleppo is renowned for superb pastries and rich desserts.

Syria produces fruity wines similar to those of the Lebanon. *Arak* is drunk with *mezze*. Traditional fruit juices – tamarind, orange and pomegranate – are losing ground to bottled soft drinks. Tea is drunk at every opportunity. Coffee is always served with a large glass of water to quench the thirst. Yogurt-and-water is drunk by the Bedouin.

Several Jordanian dishes have roots in Bedouin cooking. The best example is *mansaf*, meaning "the large tray" or dish on which this traditional repast is served. A vast communal dinner, *mansaf* consists of slices of stewed mutton, rice, bread, and *jameed* (a dried sheep's milk yogurt crumbled, melted, and poured over the food). Similar to the Arab *khouzi*, *mansaf* is served on the floor of a tent with everyone sitting around the dish helping themselves.

Fatir is another popular food, consisting of unleavened bread soaked in yogurt and topped with *samneh*, or clarified butter.

In Amman, *mezze* are popular: variations are *kishki*, or yogurt mixed with chopped walnuts and olive oil and sprinkled with the lemony spice known as *sumak*. Most *mezze* are an extension of Lebanese cuisine.

Soups are not widespread, perhaps because of the rich sauces that accompany many main courses. Soups made from lentils, meat and vegetables and *frieka* (cracked smoked wheat) are most common, especially in the western escarpment overlooking the Dead Sea.

Popular main courses are *yakneh* (a meat and vegetable casserole), *mahshi* or stuffed vegetables, chicken and *kebabs*. *Shawarma* (sliced lamb on a skewer) is as popular in Jordan as it is in Syria or Lebanon.

Like poultry, meat is marinated to tenderize it and to absorb flavors. A common custom adds cilantro fried with garlic to many recipes: a small wooden mortar and pestle used solely for grinding this mixture is kept in every kitchen. Common vegetables in Jordanian cooking are tomatoes, okra, cabbage and eggplants. Rice is more popular as a side dish there than in Syria or Lebanon, a custom linked to basic Bedouin cooking.

There are even delicatessens in America that specialize in *knaffeh*, a cream-cheese dessert with Palestinian origins. Most local desserts and confectioneries are made throughout the Levant.

Bread is eaten with every meal with many variations on the common, rounded, unleavened pocket bread known simply as *khoubz*. People buy *ka'ik bil sim-sim*, a soft bread ring sprinkled with sesame seeds, that is sold with a boiled egg and a tiny package of spices, to eat on their way to work.

TURKEY
Ottoman domination of the Middle East had a big influence on ethnic cooking. Many recipes have Turkish origins: who but the Turks would call dishes "Dainty Fingers" or "Lady's Thighs" – *kadin budu*?

The Ottoman sultans' opulent tastes also extended to the kitchen. The largest parts of the Topkapi Palace were the kitchens, where we are told that about sixty chefs and two hundred assistants devised special delicacies. It is said they had at least forty ways of cooking eggplant and more than sixty ways of making *baklava*. There were specialists for *böreks* (stuffed pastries), cooks for fish, meat and poultry, and pastry bakers.

Based on meat and dairy products, Turkish food is high in protein. Plain yogurt is greatly enjoyed, blended into soups and sauces or as a flavoring in cakes. White cheese is always found in a *meze* (*mezze*) with other appetizers.

Seafood is popular on the coast, while lamb is the basic meat. The *döner kebap* (turning kabob) has traveled to the far corners of the earth with Turkish migrants. *Döner kebap* (*shawarma* in Arabic) slowly turning on a skewer is a familiar sight. Pieces of lamb are loaded onto a vertical skewer that slowly turns in front of an electric broiler. As they cook, they are sliced into a tray or, if a customer is waiting, into a pocket of *ekmek* (pita bread) that is filled with salad.

Turkish cooks perform miracles with the most mundane vegetables. Plain by most standards, the cabbage is elevated to regal status by stuffing it with rice, raisins and pine nuts. The stuffed eggplant dish *Imam bayıldı* (swooning Imam) has captured the imagination of cooks all over the world. Rice is habitually served with main courses; Turks like long-grain rice cooked so that a little moisture remains.

Desserts are those based on milk, such as *muhallabia*, or rice pudding, and those made from pastry such as *baklava*. The most famous confectionery is *lokum*, known popularly as "Turkish Delight."

Traditional beverages are beer, wine and *rakı (arak)*. Made from grapes and aniseed, *raki* clouds when water is added, giving it the popular name of *Aslan sutu*, or "lion's milk." Other drinks are *aryan* (yogurt and water) and *shira*, or grape juice. Turkish coffee is served *şekersiz* (without surgar), *orta şekerli* (medium) or *şerkerli* (plenty of sugar).

EGYPT

The origins of some Egyptian recipes can be traced back to Pharaonic times. It is fascinating to consider that *bamieh*, or okra stew, and *melokhia* leaf soup were as popular then as they are today, but it is a disappointment not to find a grand dish that epitomizes the best of Egyptian cooking.

Most Egyptian recipes contain elements from the whole range of food generally thought of as Middle Eastern fare, while the *couscous* of north Africa is popular. Occupying armies have also influenced the local repertoire, and whether the famous *Umm Ali* pudding is actually British or Egyptian is something of a moot question.

The peasant dish *foul medames* (brown bean casserole) is eaten by three-quarters of the population before work.

While most middle-class Egyptian households serve *mezze*, they do not reach the elaborate proportions of the Levant. Eaten dipped in *tahini, falafel* (ground fava-bean patties) are a great favorite.

Poultry is greatly prized. In Old Cairo, you will see pigeon cages suspended from the windows. Famous for nightclubs, Kasr el Nil, the long avenue leading to the Giza Pyramids, has several restaurants which specialize in roast pigeon. A variety of Egyptian and other Middle Eastern dishes are served in the Khan el-Kalili Restaurant in the heart of Cairo's great bazaar.

The Nile Valley produces wonderful vegetables. Citrus fruits are plentiful, the round green lime having a special place in local cooking. Fruit juices – grape, orange and lemon, tamarind and mango – are popular, and tea is widely drunk.

Popular desserts are *Umm Ali* and *muhallabia*, while an old family cook who used to work for the British is sure to produce a good pudding. *Baklava* and *basbousa* are among many sweet pastries. Groppi's tearoom in Cairo is a popular rendezvous for tea and pastries.

ARAB STATES

Apart from Yemen, the cooking is similar throughout Arabia (Saudi Arabia, Bahrain, Kuwait, Qatar, the United Arab Emirates and the Sultanate of Oman). Prior to the wealth from oil and gas deposits, the Arabs lived on a Bedouin diet of dates, rice, and meat when it was available. The coastal communities also ate fish.

All the Arab states enjoy splendid seafood. While the souks and supermarkets are stocked with everything money can buy, some countries have become self-sufficient in certain foods, thus increasing the scope for cooking. The Gulf states grow excellent vegetables and produce milk and yogurt from cattle housed in air-conditioned stalls during the intensely hot summers.

The large number of Indians and Bangladeshis employed as cooks in the region has resulted in many dishes becoming hotter and spicier. On the coast, people are exposed to new foods in hotels. *Mezze* have become an accepted start to a meal, and a Kuwaiti or a Bahraini enjoys spaghetti just as much as an Italian.

An elaborate table setting during Eid al-fitr, the holiday following Ramadan, the month of fasting

Among themselves, most Arab families eat off a cloth spread on the living room floor. However, if a western guest is present, a table will be set with plates and silverware.

The subtle use of herbs and spices is a feature of Middle Eastern recipes. Many are native to the region, but widely available in the West.

The Arabs eat only basmati rice. Dried Indian or Omani limes are ground into a powder which, added to food, imparts an unusual, tart flavor.

Popular main courses are braised meat with potatoes, *kebabs*, fish and shrimp or chicken curries. *Khouzi* is a famous Arab dish prepared on auspicious occasions, such as a tribal wedding. In former times, the recipe called for a whole baby camel to be stuffed with a whole sheep stuffed with whole chickens, which were, in turn, stuffed with hard-boiled eggs, and the rest of the cavity stuffed with rice, nuts, raisins and spices. Today, a sheep is similarly stuffed and cooked for several hours in a huge *tanour*. When the flesh is tender, the carcass is removed and the stuffing spread on top for people to serve themselves.

Such a feast is served on the floor of the living room, or tent. V.I.P.s sit on either side of the host, who breaks off tasty pieces and passes them around. Contrary to the rather morbid western preoccupation with the Arab taste for sheep's eyes, the brains and spleen are considered the choice morsels.

Mineral water, soft drinks or yogurt drinks are common beverages. Fruit and dates are served after dinner. Oases near Nizwa, in the rugged interior of Oman, produce some of the best dates in Arabia. *Muhammar*, a sweetened rice dish, is popular.

Coffee, usually Nescafé, and sweet black tea are served afterward. *Qahwa*, coffee brewed with cardamom husks, is offered ritually on other occasions.

YEMEN

Traditional Yemeni food is unknown outside Yemen, a raggedly beautiful country with the most spectacular domestic architecture from the Middle Ages.

Local diet is based on several highly original dishes that can be attributed to the country's long isolation. Others show an Ottoman influence, while a taste for spicy foods results from contact with Indian traders on the Tihama, or Red Sea, coast.

Food is always fresh. No Yemeni housewife would dream of serving up leftovers; what is not eaten is distributed among the less fortunate. A negative side is that most dishes are served boiling hot and thus lose their nutritional value. Due to economic restraints, few dishes are very nourishing and the truly unique Yemeni recipes are unlikely to appeal to a western palate. Others common to Middle Eastern cooking – such as lentil soup and okra stew – appear in this book.

Bread is the basis of every meal; the most common is a round, unleavened bread baked from sorghum flour, which is ground by the housewife or taken to the local miller. *Bint al sahin* is a cross between bread and a pudding, eaten hot as a savory dish or smothered with *samneh* and honey.

Sheep's or goats' milk is soured by prolonged vigorous shaking in a gourd, the resulting buttermilk being used in the preparation of many dishes. Farmers in the Tihama foothills make a first-class smoked goats' milk cheese, known as *jubn*, which is sold in Ta'iz, the old capital.

Soups are popular, especially in the cooler highlands. The most common is *helba*, based on ground fenugreek seeds that are whipped to a froth with meat stock, hot pepper and other seasonings.

Similar to the Levant, dips are a tradition, but in Yemen they are different. *Zahawiq*, the best known, is made from tomatoes and chili peppers to which tiny dried fish are sometimes added. *Foul* is eaten daily. Other pulses are made into stews. *Asid* is a thick gruel-like porridge made from sorghum, boiling water, oil and honey or broth. Mutton is the most common meat, the brain and liver being especially revered.

On most days, Yemenis forego breakfast in favor of a large lunch before the *qat*-chewing session. Chewed every afternoon, the leaf depresses the appetite, so that supper, as a consequence, is late and light. On market day, breakfast is a tradition for farmers who travel long distances. Typical breakfasts are chick-peas served with fried liver, *fattah* (a dough made from dates, bananas and butter), and *mattit* (egg, tomatoes, peppers and onions made into a soup mixed with crumbled bread, butter and honey).

Most foods are cooked in vegetable oils. *Alya*, lard obtained from the melted fatty tail of sheep, is popular in rural areas. Cooking facilities remain primitive; most women cook over a fire in the kitchen or at the entrance to their house. When something special is made, it is a custom to send a portion to a neighbor.

When the meal is ready, everyone sits around the cloth unless strangers are present, in which case, women eat separately. Traditionally served first, men receive the choicest portions of food (a custom throughout the entire Middle East).

A meal is eaten in a special order. The first course is white radish, which is dipped in *helba*. A salad follows, with *bint al sahin*, soup and hot vegetable dishes such as okra and potatoes. The last course is usually mutton stew or grilled chicken with rice. This menu is typical of a middle-class urban family; most Yemenis eat a lot less.

Special foods are eaten during the holiday of Ramadan. Similar to other countries in the Middle East, the daily fast is broken with dates, grapes and other fruits, followed by a large meal. In the mountains, soups replace gruel, while *muhallabia* is a popular Ramadan dessert.

IRAN

Persian cooking is very sophisticated, a fact not generally known outside Iran. While the country has an advantage over the Arab states in being largely agricultural, local recipes display real genius in combining many unusual ingredients. A good example is meat and prune casserole. Dried fruit soups are also typically Persian.

Bread is served with every meal as an eating aid, rather than as a food to enjoy.

Salads and appetizers are essential components of a meal. Lettuce and tomato salad and cucumber salad with raisins and yogurt are very popular.

Thick yogurt is the basis of many salads, or *borani*, served as appetizers, or *pish ghaza*. Similar to *mezze*, these may consist of as many as forty small dishes and soups set out as a buffet.

Main courses cover a variety of mutton and chicken dishes, usually roasted or stewed with the addition of herbs and spices. Cooked slowly, the sauces become rich and aromatic; some become so thick that when poured over rice they make a substantial meal.

The most famous Persian dish is *chelo kebab*. The best cuts of lamb are thinly sliced and marinated in onion and lemon juice. After brief cooking over hot coals, they are arranged on a cushion of fluffy rice. Dabs of butter and a raw egg yolk are mixed into the rice, and *sumak* is sprinkled on top. Slivers of onion, radishes, and sprigs of parsley are served as garnishes. A line outside a restaurant indicates good *chelo kebab*.

The various ways of cooking rice in Iran have no equal in the Middle East; popular are steamed rice or *chelo* (see page 78) and *katteh*, a molded rice served in wedges.

The Iranian caviar fishing industry is centered in Babolsar on the Caspian Sea. The gray-green beluga caviar from the elephant sturgeon is the best quality. Sturgeon themselves are a great delicacy. The thick fillets are lightly smoked and served poached with a green lemon juice dressing. Rural restaurants serve grilled trout, while the Gulf cities enjoy good seafood in common with most Arab countries.

Desserts tend to be either rather heavy or very sweet, a general trend throughout the Middle East. Stuffed apples and quinces are very popular.

The country produces an abundance of fruit – oranges, peaches, pomegranates and succulent watermelons from the Isfahan Oasis. Many fruits are made into *sharbats*, from which the word sorbet derives.

Extolled by Farsi poets, Persian wine was of considerable quality, one of the main wine-growing regions being around Shiraz, "the city of wine and roses." *Abdug* or yogurt-and-water is drunk during a meal. People drink tea rather than coffee.

IRAQ

The art of Middle Eastern cooking reached its zenith during the Abbasid era in Baghdad – the city of Sheherezade and tales from "A Thousand and One Nights."

The culinary skills of Abbasid chefs were renowned: great chefs were presented at court, the lavishness of their creations was extolled by poets and lengthy treatises were written on the noble art of cooking. Ancient cooking manuals refer to banquets lasting for days, with table after table laden with roast partridges, ducks and francolins that had been marinated overnight in curd; milk-fed kid and spitted gazelle; and platters of desserts and confectioneries.

With the exception of one or two regional dishes, Iraqi cooking follows general trends with a historic Persian bias. While most Iraqis eat sparingly, when they do eat, the meal resembles a last supper. An Iraqi dining table is invariably loaded with exotic food.

Appetizers are usually stuffed potatoes, *dolmas* and salads. Spiked with mint, yogurt is popular, while rice dishes are similar to Persian varieties. The most elaborate, *timman za'fran*, includes ground meat, raisins and nuts – a substantial meal.

A variation on the famous Saudi *khouzi* steams a whole lamb on a domestic stove, then barbecues it over a bed of rice in a *tanour*. Suspended head down, the fatty tail constantly bastes the carcass as it melts.

Parks and gardens line the Tigris River flowing through Baghdad, where restaurants are set out under the trees. A traditional dish is *mashgouf*, a delicious fish that is slowly smoked over an open fire and served with sliced tomatoes, onions and bread.

Fish and dates are twin products in Basra, at the head of the Persian Gulf. Dates have a myriad of uses – barbecued fish with date purée is typical of Basra; dates are made into *halwa*, a toffee-like dessert, and stuffed in pastries.

Mentioned in the *Arabian Nights*, the sweet, orange-colored rosettes known as *zlabiya* are still popular.

Dessert and coffee are served in the living room. If people have used their fingers to eat, a servant may bring a pitcher of water and soap to wash. Most urban houses have western-style bathrooms.

ETIQUETTE, CUSTOMS AND COOKING TIPS

Living an isolated existence in the desert, Bedouin nomads display the same characteristics as an American family in the Midwest or Australians in the Outback. Hospitality is second nature: while having no idea from where their next meal may come, they will offer what they have – their last bread or dates. In extending their hospitality, reflected in the coffee ceremony (see pages 141 to 142), they consider it their duty to protect a guest, even a complete stranger. As more and more Bedouin exchange nomadism for a sedentary life, these same unwritten rules apply in the city.

There are certain rules of etiquette in the Middle East which *Orientales*, as people call themselves, have observed since the revelations of the holy *Quran*. "Cleanliness is next to godliness" is a saying that may have come from Muslim society. It is unthinkable not to wash before saying your prayers or sitting down to eat. Even basic Arab restaurants have a corner basin. Incense is frequently burned to purify the air.

A strict code of etiquette at mealtime expresses subtle distinctions among the diners. An important guest will be offered special delicacies, such as the tail of the chicken and so on. The host has the first taste, a custom to show the food is worthy of being eaten and to encourage others to eat.

A meal always commences with thanks to Allah, the provider – *bismillah!* Morsels of food are given or accepted using only the right hand. You should never

An elaborate silver tamarind juice stand in Damascus, Syria.

A village baker and his young sister in Iran. The huge, long loaves of bread hang outside his bakery.

refuse pieces offered by your host, because it is considered impolite. If seated on the floor, the soles of the feet must not be displayed as this, too, is considered ill-mannered. Other aspects of local etiquette are similar to western table manners: not to fill your mouth too full, not to finish eating first in order not to embarrass others.

DIETARY LAWS

Muslim dietary laws are prescribed in the *Quran*, the book of revelations revealed to the Prophet Muhammed by the Angel Gabriel in seventh-century Arabia and later transcribed by his companions.

Food is frequently mentioned, the major rules being abstention from eating the flesh of swine, the blood of any animal, or even eating any animal that has not been slaughtered in the correct manner by a Muslim (*hilal*). Muslims slit the throat of a beast while repeating the phrase: "In the name of God, God is most great!" Alcoholic drinks are forbidden.

SPICES

Middle Eastern food is characterized by the subtle use of spices bought in the *attarine*, or spice street, where traders squat in tiny stores among boxes of colorful spices.

While today the emphasis is on the value of spices as flavoring, they have always had uses as homeopathic remedies, as vegetable dyes and in purification rituals.

Cassia and cinnamon were essential components in Egyptian embalming oils. Frankincense and cinnamon were among the gifts taken by the Queen of Sheba on her historic journey to Jerusalem. Frankincense and myrrh were also offered to the infant Jesus in Bethlehem.

Contact with the East inevitably introduced spices to western kitchens: crusading knights brought new ideas for flavoring; and the use of spices in Abbasid society was second to none.

The following spices are commonly used in Middle Eastern cooking:

A native of the Middle East, anise is cultivated for its small, oil-bearing seeds. Allspice is a fragrant spice, like a blend of cinnamon, nutmeg, and cloves. It is used in stuffings.

The Middle East is the world's biggest importer of cardamom, whose crushed seeds are blended into meat dishes, while whole pods flavor desserts and coffee.

While paprika is used in many regions, hotter spices such as chili powder are generally restricted to the Yemen. Cinnamon is used in a variety of dishes, while cloves are used to flavor veal and other dishes. Coriander is another native spice, which Mesopotamian records claim was cultivated in the fabled hanging gardens of Babylon.

Cumin, the "queen of spices," is also a native of the Middle East. Its delicate aroma complements many vegetable dishes and salads – *falafel* need a good pinch of cumin to enliven their flavor. Used ground or whole, cumin is an ingredient in Gulf fish curries. Ground fenugreek seeds help thicken curries and are excellent served with potatoes and eggplants.

Ginger appears in many medieval recipes, its medicinal value being noted in the *Quran*. Ginger tea is a soothing beverage. Abbasid society used nutmeg as a remedy for intestinal disorders; today it is used as a flavor and decoration for desserts.

The world's most popular spice, pepper, is used to flavor savory dishes, and if pepper tops the popularity poll, then saffron is the world's most expensive spice. It requires over 250,000 crocus stigmas to make a pound of saffron but only a few strands to give a beautiful glow to rice and poultry dishes. Turmeric, a yellow Indian spice, is a cheaper alternative but no substitute in terms of flavor.

Sesame seed is historically a valuable spice in the Middle East. Raw or roasted, its seeds flavor many dishes and breads. Sesame seed oil is used on salads and in cooking.

FESTIVALS

There are several important religious festivals in the Muslim calendar.

Eid al-fitr is observed in the tenth month, following Ramadan, the month of fasting, when fasting from dawn until dusk is considered good self-discipline and spiritually uplifting. It begins when the new moon is sighted over Mecca, in Saudi Arabia. Special desserts are made for the celebrations; *nahash*, a cream cheese and phyllo pastry, is a Syrian specialty made at this time.

COOKING UTENSILS

Being very old, most of the recipes in this book were originally cooked using unsophisticated utensils on primitive stoves. A modern person cooking the Middle Eastern way needs only three or four basic items in addition to normal kitchen utensils: a large, deep skillet, preferably made of cast iron; a mortar and pestle; and a blender or food processor.

COOKING INGREDIENTS

Cooking oils are basically vegetable oils, such as corn oil and sunflower oil, or various nut oils. Dishes to be eaten cold are made with olive oil, which is the foundation for all dressings.

Samneh is melted butter, clarified by straining the oil through a thin piece of cheesecloth, which extracts any impurities to impart a richer taste. Like *alya, samneh* is mainly used in rural communities.

Other items to have in stock for cooking the Middle Eastern way are *bulghur*, or cracked wheat; *tahina* or *tahini*, sesame seed paste; *phyllo* pastry; flavorings such as orange-flower and rose waters; and a supply of almonds, pine nuts, walnuts and pistachios.

Spice names

The following are Arabic translations of the most commonly used spices – a handy guide for shopping in the souks:

Allspice: *bahar*	Ginger: *zanjibil*
Anise: *anisun*	Mace: *fuljan*
Black pepper: *fil-fil afwad*	Nutmeg: *jawz al-teeb*
Cardamom: *hayl (hababan)*	Paprika: *fil-fil ahmar*
Chili: *fil-fil ahmar har*	Saffron: *za'fran*
Cloves: *kabsh qaranful*	Sesame seed: *sim-sim*
Coriander: *kusbarah*	Tamarind: *tammar*
Cumin: *kammun*	*al-Hindi*
Fenugreek: *helba*	Tumeric: *kurkum*

Making a pita-bread sandwich in a Cairo snackbar.

PAGES 22 AND 23   *A large mezze table may include up to 70 small dishes.*

Mezze

Even damaged by war, Beirut remains an enchanting city that many other places on the Mediterranean have tried to emulate but without success. Standing with its feet in the sea and with its back to snow-capped mountains, it is sophisticated and fun-loving. Here you will always eat well, and the nightclubs in Jounieh offer some of the best cabaret acts in the Middle East.

I first visited Lebanon in 1970 to write some travel articles. In the late Seventies, I returned to photograph the war-torn city for *The Times* (of London). And in 1993 I went back to find Beirut is on its feet again – life is normal, the shops are busy and restaurants are full.

On my initial visit, a friend and I chose to eat in a restaurant at Pigeon Grotto, which remains a popular family outing on the seafront. Having ordered *mezze*, we were choosing a main course when the *maître d'hôtel* suggested that *mezze* would probably suffice. Imagine our relief, therefore, when plate after plate of appetizers was brought to the table. Counted, they numbered twenty-five and were obviously a meal.

Essentially a Lebanese creation, *mezze* assume the aura of a banquet when prepared by a cook of repute. A way of life in Lebanon, Syria and Turkey, *mezze* have been adopted by other countries in the Middle East. As many as seventy dishes may be served in a large *mezze* on an auspicious occasion such as a marriage.

Items may be miniatures of a main course or true *hors d'oeuvres*, similar to a Scandinavian *smörgasbord*. Their preparation is time-consuming, but many *mezze* can be made beforehand and chilled. Others, such as sautéed testicles, should be served fresh for best results. Ideally, you need someone to help, either to cook or to take the dishes to the table.

You can plan *mezze* around whatever you like, but there are about a dozen basic items without which even a small *mezze* is incomplete. First, the *mezze* table must always have a basket of freshly baked bread, the round, unleavened bread known vaguely as *khoubz Arabieh*, which is used instead of silverware to scoop up food. It is also essential for the dips.

Three or four dips are always found on a *mezze* table. The best known is *hummus*, a creamy, pale yellow dip made from mashed chick-peas and *tahini* (a paste made from ground sesame seeds), blended with lemon juice and spices. Also popular is *babagannouj*, a pleasant, smoky-tasting dip made from grilled mashed eggplant, garlic and *tahini*. I love it, one dish of *babagannouj* never being enough as I sit talking, dipping bread in it.

Taramasalata is flesh-colored purée made from dried and salted gray mullet, or, commonly, from cod. Bread and celery sticks are dipped into *taramasalata*, which is now so popular you can buy it in some supermarkets, although the very best is homemade. Made from strained yogurt, thick, creamy *labneh* is always part of a *mezze*. In contrast, a purée of red pepper and walnuts, *muhammara*, is a hot dip. Both keep well in the refrigerator.

Another familiar constituent of *mezze* is stuffed grape leaves. These are popular throughout the Middle East, served either hot, with a ground meat filling, or cold, stuffed with rice and pine nuts.

Lebanese cooking suffers from only one handicap in that there is no good beef available. This is true throughout the Middle East, where nowhere is a cattle-raising country. As mutton is also frequently of poor quality, a great many seasonings are used to compensate for the lack of flavor, and meat is often ground to disguise the tough texture. Usually there are at least two ground meat dishes in a basic *mezze*. *Kibbeh nayé* consists of raw, seasoned ground lamb that is combined with other ingredients, shaped into meatballs and fried.

Strips of fried liver and *sanbusak* or *börek* (pastries) filled with ground meat, cream cheese and spinach are also popular *mezze*. Artichoke hearts, brains (both with lemon and olive oil dressing), cubes of white cheese, celery, olives and pickled sweet peppers are easy-to-serve cold dishes. And I could go on endlessly listing more dishes –*falafel* (dried and mashed white fava bean patties, or croquettes), fried mussels, chicken wings broiled with garlic and yogurt sauce, miniature pizzas . . .

But, finally, there is *tabbouleh*, the Lebanese national salad, without which no *mezze* is complete. Very refreshing, it has a crunchy texture from the cracked wheat and a tangy taste from the lemon. It must be served fresh.

By tradition, *mezze* are eaten with *arak* (*raki* in Turkey), a spirit similar to *pastis* drinks like Pernod.

Kadin Budu   "Lady's thighs"

*1 pound lean ground beef or
    lamb*

2 eggs

¼ cup rice

1 teaspoon olive oil

*1 medium onion, finely
    chopped*

*2½ tablespoons very finely
    chopped parsley*

salt and pepper

flour, to coat

½ cup butter

SERVES ABOUT 4

First cook the rice as for Plain *pilav* rice (page 78) until just under-done (test a grain with your teeth). Set aside to cool.

Knead the meat well in a large bowl, then add one of the eggs, the cool rice, oil, chopped onion and parsley. Season and mix together very well to form a smooth paste.

With moistened hands, break off lumps of the mixture and shape into walnut-sized balls. Place in a skillet with 1 cup of water and simmer gently for 15 minutes. Drain and set aside to cool.

Beat the remaining egg and dip the meatballs in it, then roll them in flour. Fry them in the melted butter over a high heat until they are crisp and brown. Keep warm until ready to serve. Good *kadin budu* should be crispy with a juicy interior.

Babagannouj   Eggplant dip

2 large eggplants
4 tablespoons tahini *(sesame seed paste)*
juice of 1 lemon
2 cloves garlic, crushed
salt and pepper, to taste
1 teaspoon finely chopped parsley, to garnish
olive oil, to serve

SERVES ABOUT 4

Slit the skins of the eggplants – this allows the steam to escape during cooking – then bake or broil gently until the outsides are charred and crisp and they begin to split. Cut them in half, scoop out the flesh and mash thoroughly.

Combine with the *tahini*, lemon juice, garlic, salt and pepper and process or blend to a smooth consistency. If the mixture seems too thick, add some water, which will turn it a whiter color.

Serve in a glass or pottery dish garnished with the chopped parsley. Pour a teaspoon of olive oil into the center.

Babagannouj is most often eaten as a dip with pita bread, but it can also be served as a salad with ripe olives and tomato slices.

Hummus   Chick-pea dip

1 cup dried chick-peas
1 teaspoon salt
1 to 2 garlic cloves, crushed
salt
⅔ cup tahini (sesame seed paste)
juice of 2 to 3 lemons
1 tablespoon olive oil
paprika, to sprinkle (optional)
finely chopped parsley, to
*   garnish (optional)*

SERVES ABOUT 6

Soak the chick-peas in plenty of cold water overnight. Drain, add the salt, cover with water and cook in a pressure cooker for about 20 minutes, or simmer for 1½ hours in a pan. Drain the chick-peas, reserving the liquid, then set aside a few peas for garnish.

Using a little of the cooking liquid, reduce the rest of the chick-peas to a purée in a blender or food processor. Add the garlic, salt and *tahini*, and blend together thoroughly. Pour in the lemon,

juice, by which time the *hummus* should have a rich, creamy consistency.

Pour into a shallow, concave dish (about the size of a salad plate), pour the oil in the center and garnish with the whole chick-peas. Sprinkle the paprika and a little chopped parsley as a decoration around the edges, if you like.

Hummus should be served at room temperature as a dip with warmed pita bread. It also makes an ideal accompaniment to grilled *kebabs*.

Taramasalata   Fish roe dip

4 slices thick, stale white bread
4 tablespoons cold milk
4 ounces fish roe (see method)
1 clove garlic, crushed
½ small onion, finely minced
juice of 1 to 2 lemons, to taste
1 egg yolk
4 tablespoons olive oil

SERVES ABOUT 4

The most authentic roe to use is *tarama*, the dried and salted roe of the gray mullet. Smoked cod's roe can be used instead, in which case the skins will need to be removed first.

Remove the crusts and soak the bread in the cold milk. Meanwhile, pound the roe thoroughly in a mortar or purée in a food processor until it is soft.

Squeeze the bread dry and crumble it into the roe. Add the garlic and onion, half the lemon juice and pound (or blend) to a

creamy paste. When it is smooth, break in the egg yolk and continue to pound or blend while dribbling in the olive oil and the rest of the lemon juice.

Chill and serve as a dip with whole radishes, ripe olives, celery sticks and pita bread.

Most *taramasalata* sold commercially is artificially colored and tastes nothing like this authentic recipe. The homemade version will keep for about 10 days in a sealed container in the refrigerator.

Tahini   Sesame paste dip

2 cloves garlic
salt, to taste
juice of 2 large lemons
6 tablespoons tahini (sesame
*   seed paste)*
pinch of ground cumin
1 teaspoon finely chopped
*   parsley*

SERVES ABOUT 4

Crush the garlic and salt together. Mix with a little lemon juice and blend with the *tahini*. Add the cumin and remaining lemon juice to form a smooth paste, like peanut butter.

Use more garlic if you want the *tahini* to taste stronger. If it is too thick, reduce it with water. As with *hummus*, a blender is ideal for making *tahini*: the result will be smoother and creamier than if made by hand. Serve in a bowl and garnish with the parsley.

A selection of Middle Eastern dips often included as part of a mezze *–* Hummus *(top),* Tahini *(center) and* Taramasalata.

Labneh Thick yogurt

1¼ cups plain yogurt
salt, to taste
finely chopped fresh mint, to
   garnish
olive oil

SERVES ABOUT 4

Most mezze *tables will include a selection of dips, including these. Creamy white* labneh *is a wholesome yogurt dip.* Muhammara *(recipe, page 30) is a hot dip excellent with grilled and broiled meats. Serve both with pita bread (page 41).*

Fold a large piece of damp cheesecloth in half, and place over a large bowl. Pour the yogurt into the middle of the cloth, tie the cloth corners together with string and suspend over the bowl overnight.

Remove the yogurt from the cloth, tip into another bowl, stir in salt to taste and chill. Garnish with chopped fresh mint and a trickle of olive oil in the center.

Labneh will keep for one week in a sealed container in the refrigerator. Serve with pita bread as a dip. In many Middle Eastern countries, it is eaten with olives for breakfast.

Dolma   Stuffed grape leaves

*50 fresh grape leaves, or 12
    ounces grape leaves
    preserved in brine, well
    rinsed*

1 cup long-grain rice

liberal pinch of salt

1 large onion, finely chopped

2 cloves garlic, crushed

2 teaspoons finely chopped mint

*2 tablespoons finely chopped
    parsley*

pinch of ground allspice

freshly ground black pepper

3 tablespoons olive oil

*1 pound finely ground lamb or
    beef*

juice of 1 to 2 lemons

lemon slices, to garnish

2 cups chicken stock

butter

SERVES ABOUT 10

Cut the stems off the grape leaves. If using
fresh leaves, blanch single leaves in
boiling water for 2 to 3 minutes, then place
in a bowl of cold water to stop the cooking.
If using preserved leaves, place them in a
large bowl. Cover with boiling water and
leave to soak for 10 to 15 minutes. Place
the leaves in cold water and ease the
leaves apart. Drain well.

Boil the rice in salted water until just
tender, then rinse under cold running
water and set aside to drain.

Meanwhile, sauté the onion, garlic,
herbs and seasonings in the oil. Add the
meat and toss until lightly browned.
Remove from heat and leave to cool, then
add the rice, mixing everything together
very well.

To shape, place a drained grape leaf on
a work surface, shiny side down, and

sprinkle with a drop of lemon juice. Place
about 1 tablespoon of the meat mixture
near the stem end, then fold in the end and
sides and roll up neatly. Repeat this
process until all the leaves are stuffed.

Line the bottom of a large, heavy-based
roasting pan with several grape leaves,
then arrange the filled rolls in stacks with
lemon slices between. Pour in the stock,
add dabs of butter on the top and cover
with any remaining leaves, or with
aluminum foil. Place a heatproof dish on
the top to keep the rolls pressed down,
cover with a lid and simmer slowly for 1 to
2 hours, or until the leaves are tender.

Serve the *dolma* lukewarm, sprinkled
with lemon juice. Alternatively, you may
prefer to serve with a garlic, olive oil and
lemon juice dressing. Garnish with halved
lemon slices.

Muhammara Hot-pepper dip

2 medium onions, finely
  chopped
6 tablespoons olive oil
¾ cup walnut pieces, finely
  chopped
1 cup fresh bread crumbs
  blended with cold water to a
  purée
1 tablespoon paprika, or ½
  teaspoon chili powder for a
  very hot muhammara, or 1
  small can hot-pepper paste
a pinch of ground cumin
salt
1 tablespoon pine nuts sautéed
  in a little oil

SERVES ABOUT 6

Using a deep skillet, sauté the onions gently in the oil until soft and golden. Add the walnuts, the bread-crumb purée, the paprika (or chili or hot-pepper paste), the cumin and salt to taste. Continue to sauté gently over low heat until the ingredients are well blended, about 12 minutes.

Remove from the heat, place in a bowl and garnish with the pine nuts.

Muhammara is eaten as a dip with bread. It can also be used as a spicy dip with *kebabs* and grilled meats and fish. The Lebanese also eat it as a spread on toast.

Falafel Fava bean patties

2⅔ cups dried fava beans
6 scallions, finely chopped
3 cloves garlic, crushed
6 tablespoons finely chopped
  parsley
1 teaspoon ground cumin
1 teaspoon very finely chopped
  fresh cilantro
salt and cayenne pepper
oil for deep frying
lemon wedges, to garnish
  (optional)

SERVES ABOUT 6

Soak the beans overnight in plenty of cold water. The next day, drain, and then skin them. Grind in a food processor, or pound in a mortar.

Add all the other ingredients (except for the oil) and blend or pound to a smooth pastelike consistency. Leave to stand, uncovered, for 15 minutes, then chill. The paste will dry out in the refrigerator and the *falafel* will be easier to handle.

With moistened hands, take small lumps, flatten slightly to form a ball shape and place on a tray. Prepare the remaining bean mixture in this manner.

Heat ½-inch oil in a deep skillet and fry the patties, turning frequently until they are golden brown. Drain well on paper towels and serve garnished with lemon wedges, if you like. *Falafel* are traditionally eaten with a side dish of *tahini* dip.

Falafel *are crunchy spiced bean patties. A popular Egyptian snack, they are usually eaten dipped in* tahini *(page 26).*

Tabbouleh   Lebanese "national" salad

1¹/₃ *cups* bulghur *(cracked wheat)*
1 cup finely chopped onion
1 tablespoon chopped fresh mint
8 tablespoons chopped parsley
2 medium tomatoes, skinned and diced
1 x 2-inch piece cucumber, diced
salt and pepper, to taste
3 tablespoons olive oil
3 tablespoons lemon juice
ripe olives, to garnish

SERVES 6

Soak the *bulghur* in cold water for 1 hour before preparing the salad. Drain it and squeeze out the moisture using your hands. Pat dry on a cloth.

Place it in a bowl with the onion and mix together well. Add the mint, parsley, tomato, cucumber, seasonings, oil and lemon juice, and blend together well. Above all, *tabbouleh* should have a distinctive lemony flavor. (I recommend skinning the tomatoes before you chop them, but it isn't necessary. It just depends if you have time or not.)

Serve the salad chilled, in a glass dish, decorated with a few ripe olives. *Tabbouleh* is eaten scooped up in bread or, more traditionally, in lettuce leaves.

Artichoke Hearts in Olive Oil

6 small fresh artichokes
6 tablespoons lemon juice
2 cloves garlic, halved
6 tablespoons olive oil
salt and pepper

SERVES 4

Remove the stem and outer leaves of each artichoke and drop the hearts into a bowl of cold water acidulated with a few drops of lemon juice.

Place the hearts in a heavy pan with 1¾ cups water, half the quantities of lemon juice and olive oil and the garlic. Season with salt and pepper, then bring to a boil.

Simmer, uncovered, until the hearts are tender, 20 to 30 minutes.

Remove the hearts from the liquid and cool. Mix the rest of the oil and lemon juice with half the remaining liquid, and add more seasoning to taste. Pour over the hearts, cover with plastic wrap and chill until you are ready to eat. Serve cold.

33

Sanbusak   Stuffed crescent pastries

4 tablespoons butter
1 cup vegetable oil
1 cup water
1 teaspoon salt
3 cups all-purpose flour
egg yolk or milk, to glaze

MAKES ABOUT 20

To make the dough, melt the butter gently and pour into a glass bowl. Add the oil, water and salt and stir well.

Add the flour, 1 tablespoon at a time, mixing it in thoroughly. Any lumps will gradually disappear. The consistency is correct when pieces of dough flake off the sides of the bowl, and you can form a ball of smooth dough in your hands.

While you are stuffing the *sanbusaks* (see right), preheat the oven to 350°F.

To make a *sanbusak*, break off a ball of dough, and roll to a circle of about

3 inches in diameter. Put 1 teaspoon of the filling on one half of the circle, taking care not to overfill (the mixture expands during the baking), and fold the other half over the filling.

Close the sides of the dough well by crimping with your fingers and thumb. Continue until all the dough and filling are used up.

Lay each *sanbusak* side by side on a baking sheet, glaze with a little egg yolk or milk, and bake until golden brown, about 30 minutes.

Cheese filling

½ pound feta cheese,
*   crumbled*
pepper
2 hard-boiled eggs, diced
3 tablespoons chopped parsley
*   or chives*

Mix the ingredients together to form a paste and stuff the *sanbusak* as described. It is not necessary to use salt with a salty white cheese such as feta.

Meat filling

1 medium onion, finely
*   chopped*
⅓ cup pine nuts, chopped
2 tablespoons butter
½ pound lean ground lamb
pinch of ground allspice
salt and pepper to taste

Sauté the onion and nuts in the butter until golden. Add the meat, salt, pepper and allspice, and cook gently until the meat changes color, about 10 minutes. Remove from the pan and cool. Use to stuff the *sanbusak* as described.

Spinach filling

1 pound fresh spinach
1 medium onion, finely
*   chopped*
olive oil for frying
salt and white pepper
pinch of paprika
¾ cup crumbled feta cheese

Remove and discard stems and large veins from the spinach, then wash, drain and chop the leaves finely.

Sauté the onion in a little oil until soft and golden. Add the spinach, seasonings and cheese and mix together well. Cook until tender. Leave to cool, then mix in the cheese before stuffing the *sanbusaks* as described.

Brains in Lemon and Olive Oil Dressing

4 sets lambs' brains
3 tablespoons vinegar
salt and white pepper, to taste
1/2 onion, sliced
1/2 lemon, sliced
juice of 1 1/2 to 2 lemons
4 1/2 tablespoons olive oil
1/2 clove garlic, crushed
2 tablespoons finely chopped
    parsley
lemon wedges and extra
    parsley, to garnish

SERVES 4

Soak the brains for 1 hour in water to cover with 2 tablespoons of the vinegar. Rinse under running water, then remove all the membranes and gray tissues.

Place the brains in a saucepan with the remaining 1 tablespoon vinegar and warm water to cover. Add salt, onion and lemon slices and simmer gently over low heat for about 15 minutes.

Remove the pan from the heat and drain the brains, then set aside to cool. Chill for 2 to 3 hours in a refrigerator.

Slice the brains into quarters. Blend together the lemon juice, olive oil, garlic and parsley together and pour over the brains. Serve them chilled with lemon wedges and a garnish of more parsley.

Fried Liver

1 pound lambs' or calves' liver
salt and pepper
1 clove garlic, crushed
pinch of paprika
2 tablespoons butter
3 tablespoons lemon juice
parsley, to garnish

SERVES ABOUT 4

Slice the liver into 1/4-inch thick strips. Pat dry on paper towels.

Rub the salt, pepper and garlic into the liver strips, then sprinkle them with paprika.

Melt the butter and add lemon juice. Add the liver and cook over high heat for about 30 seconds on each side. Transfer to a dish and serve immediately, garnished with the parsley.

Beid Ghanam   Sautéed lambs' testicles

about 1/2 pound lambs' testicles
vinegar
1 clove garlic, crushed
1/2 cup butter
1/2 teaspoon Italian seasoning
salt and white pepper
juice of 1 lemon
finely chopped parsley, to
    garnish

SERVES ABOUT 4

To clean the testicles, first remove the outer skin by slicing the sac and pushing the testicles out. Separate the sac by cutting the connected duct. Discard the sac and rinse the testicles under cold water. Soak for 1 hour in water with 2 tablespoons of vinegar. Drain, remove any veins and chop.

Sauté the crushed garlic in melted butter, then add the herbs, salt and pepper. Cook the testicles lightly in the butter until golden brown. Do not overcook. Finally add the lemon juice and serve hot, garnished with chopped parsley.

Some of the more unusual delicacies included in many Middle Eastern mezze: *Brains in lemon and olive oil dressing (top); Fried liver (middle); and* Beid ghanam, *or sautéed lambs' testicles.*

*Chicken wings spiked with garlic
and lemon juice can be served hot
or cold*

Chicken Wings with Garlic and Yogurt

8 chicken wings, cut in half
6 tablespoons lemon juice
2 cloves garlic, crushed
1 teaspoon paprika
salt and white pepper
¾ cup plain yogurt
garden cress or parsley, to
    garnish

SERVES ABOUT 4

Marinate the wings in lemon juice with crushed garlic and seasonings for 1 hour, turning occasionally. Remove and drain.

Mix the yogurt into the marinade, then brush onto the wings. Place under a medium-hot broiler. As the yogurt dries, brush more on. The wings should become brown and crisp. Serve warm, garnished with garden cress or parsley.

Fried Mussels

40 large mussels
oil for deep frying
flour for coating
lemon slices and parsley, to
    garnish

Batter
2 envelopes active-dry yeast
½ cup lukewarm water, or
    enough to make the
    consistency of light cream
pinch of sugar
salt
¾ cup all-purpose flour, sifted
1½ tablespoons oil

Tarator sauce
2 slices stale white bread, soaked
    in water and squeezed dry
½ cup ground blanched
    almonds or pine nuts
2 cloves garlic, crushed
juice of 1 lemon
6 tablespoons olive oil
salt and pepper, to taste

White sauce
3½ tablespoons butter
salt and pepper
2 tablespoons flour
about 1 cup milk
good pinch of mace

SERVES 6

Make the batter first and leave it to stand while preparing the *tarator* sauce, the white sauce and the mussels. Dissolve the yeast in the water with the sugar and salt. When it has frothed, mix into the flour with the oil. The batter should have the consistency of gloss paint.

Mix together all the *tarator* ingredients with a mortar and pestle until they form a creamy paste.

For the white sauce, melt the butter in a small saucepan with salt and pepper. Stir in the flour using a wooden spoon, adding the milk gradually and stirring all the time. Add enough milk so the sauce becomes sloppy without being thick. Set aside and keep warm.

Wash the mussels under running water and, using a brush and knife, remove beards and any barnacles. Discard any that are open. Make sure any sand or grit is thoroughly rinsed off.

Boil the mussels vigorously in salted water until the shells open, about 5 minutes. Discard any that have not opened. Leave the mussels to cool, then remove them from their shells and place on a board. Retain the mussel stock.

Heat the oil in a deep pan. Coat each mussel with white sauce, then dip it in the flour and then the batter. Drop into the sizzling oil, and deep-fry until crisp and golden, about 1 minute.

Drain and serve immediately on a plate garnished with fresh parsley and lemon slices with a side dish of *tarator* sauce. Spear the mussels with toothpicks and dip them into the sauce.

In the West, mayonnaise or tartar sauce might be served with these fried mussels.

Mussels fried in batter are common mezze in Lebanon and Turkey.

Pickled Chili Peppers

1 pound long, mild chili peppers
1 small dried chili
1 ½ tablespoons salt
1 ¼ cups water
½ cup white-wine vinegar

Prick the chili peppers all over so that they absorb the marinade. Pack together tightly in a large glass jar with the dried chili. Add the salt, water and vinegar, ensuring that there is no air trapped between the chilies.

Seal and store for 3 weeks by which time the peppers will have softened. Remove the amount required, drain well and serve.

Khoubz Arabieh   Pita bread

1 tablespoon active-dry yeast
pinch of sugar
about 2¹/₂ cups lukewarm water
¹/₂ teaspoon salt
4 cups all-purpose flour
oil

MAKES 8

*Cool and crisp accompaniments
to pita bread – salty feta cheese,
ripe olives and pieces of celery.*

Mix the yeast and sugar into a paste with about 4 tablespoons of the water. Set aside until the mixture becomes frothy, 10 to 15 minutes.

Stir the salt into the flour in a large mixing bowl. Make a well in the center and stir in the yeast mixture with more of the water. Begin kneading into a dough, using enough water to reach a firm consistency. The dough must be well kneaded – at least 10 minutes – add a little oil if you find it is too firm at first. When the dough is smooth and elastic, shape into a ball and place in a lightly greased bowl, cover with a damp dish towel and set aside in a warm place for 1 to 2 hours, or until the dough has doubled in size.

Lightly flour your work surface. Turn out the dough onto it and punch it down until it is about ¹/₄ inch thick. Cut into 8 portions, then roll each portion into a ball and dust with flour. Cover with a dry towel and leave to rise again, about 20 minutes.

Meanwhile, preheat the oven for 15 minutes to 500°F. Grease a baking sheet and put it in the oven to heat – although be careful the oil does not burn. Using a floured wooden spatula, gently flatten each ball of dough, then lift them onto the heated baking sheet.

Sprinkle water on each to prevent it from burning, then bake for about 5 minutes until each is puffed up. The final result should be a delicate brown leaf with a soft pouch inside. Cool on a wire rack.

*Men commonly do the shopping
in many Middle Eastern societies.
Here a Kuwaiti is buying potatoes
on his way to work.*

Soups

On one of my frequent visits to Jordan, my driver took the twisting King's Highway *en route* to Petra, via Kerak, a town in the western escarpment. It was late March, and from being a sunny day, the weather suddenly turned black, lightning crackled over the Dead Sea, and wind drove sheets of hail against our windshield. Adeb and I had intended stopping only for coffee in Kerak, a town known for its lofty, crusader-built castle, but instead we lingered over a warming bowl of soup. Feast-day soup is a traditional dish, especially among Jordan's minority Christian community, of whom many live in this area and around Madaba. Dipping in chunks of bread, we found it sustained us for the rest of our journey.

While soups tend to be uncommon in the hot desert states, they are widely cooked in countries with colder climates such as Turkey, Syria and Iraq. Old Middle Eastern recipe manuals show an infinite number of meat and vegetable soups and many combinations of both.

Lentil is the most popular soup, especially in Egypt where *felaheen* may eat it three times a day. The dried pulses that are so widely cultivated in Egypt, Iraq and the Levant – lentils, fava beans, chick-peas, split peas and others – make thick, creamy soups, or *shorbah* in Arabic.

Other soups, such as vegetable soup, are so rich in ingredients that they are almost a stew and, eaten with bread, become a meal in themselves. Common vegetable soups are zucchini, carrot and a variety of spinach soups. All use fresh ingredients. .

Although I have not given the recipes, two unusual soups from Egypt and Yemen are *melokhia* and *helba*. Made with a game base and fresh *melokhia* leaves (of the mallow family and resembling mint), the first, from ancient Egyptian recipes, is still prepared almost daily by country women, the proportions varying according to their standard of living. *Helba* is a fiery soup, served scalding in earthenware bowls, that is eaten daily throughout Yemen.

Yogurt soups are a major soup category, the addition of yogurt adding a wholesome taste to any food. Often the yogurt is only added at the end, merely stirred in and gently heated. I once enjoyed a splendid yogurt soup in a small hotel in Konya, the town of whirling dervishes in central Anatolia. The Turks also use prodigious amounts of yogurt in their cooking; chilled cucumber and yogurt soup is a perfect start to lunch on a hot summer's day.

Many people will already know *avgolemono* from a Greek restaurant. The same egg and lemon soup, or *beid bi limoun* in Arabic, is common in Turkey and Lebanon. A very nourishing soup, especially for anyone who is convalescing, the recipe here is only one of many versions you will find throughout the Middle East.

Fish soups are popular along the coasts of Turkey, Syria and Lebanon. The recipe included in this chapter comes from Izmir, the Turkish port known for its annual September trade fair. Coastal restaurants in Lebanon serve wonderful *shorbat al samak* made with fresh Mediterranean fish. Iranians, as well as Iraqis, enjoy zucchini soup, a simple-to-make first course that never fails to please my guests.

The typical sweet-and-sour marriage in many sophisticated Persian dishes is found in pomegranate soup, an exotic, if time-consuming, dish to make.

A western touch with many of these soups is to garnish them with fried croutons.

Tomato Soup

2 pounds medium tomatoes
1 clove garlic, finely chopped
1 medium onion, finely chopped
pinch of ground coriander
pinch of paprika
salt and pepper, to taste
3½ tablespoons olive oil
2½ cups homemade chicken stock
juice of 1 lemon
finely chopped parsley, to garnish

SERVES 6

Scald, peel and seed the tomatoes, then chop them finely. Sauté the garlic, onion, coriander, paprika and seasonings in the olive oil until soft, then add the tomatoes and cook for 5 minutes, stirring.

Add the stock (or use half this quantity of stock made up to 2½ cups with canned tomato juice, if desired). Cover and simmer for 15 to 20 minutes. Leave the soup to cool, then purée it in a blender or food processor. Stir in the lemon juice, reheat and serve garnished with parsley.

Carrot Soup

4 tablespoons butter
1 level tablespoon ground coriander
1 pound carrots, washed, scraped and cut into
    thin slices
2½ cups chicken stock
pinch of sugar
salt and freshly ground black pepper
6 tablespoons light cream
parsley, to garnish

SERVES 4

Melt the butter in a deep skillet and stir in the coriander. Add carrots and sauté, stirring frequently, until tender, about 15 minutes. Set aside to cool.

Place the carrots in a blender or food processor with the chicken stock, sugar and salt and pepper to taste. Blend until smooth.

When ready to serve, pour the soup into a saucepan, stir in the cream and simmer until hot, but not boiling. Adjust the seasoning and garnish with parsley. This soup can be served hot or chilled.

Chilled Cucumber and Yogurt Soup

1 large cucumber
2½ cups plain yogurt
6 tablespoons fresh tomato paste
1 clove garlic, finely chopped
salt to taste
pinch of paprika, to garnish

SERVES 4

Wipe the cucumber clean, but do not peel it. Coarsely chop it, then sprinkle with salt and leave to stand for 30 minutes. Rinse and drain, and put it in a blender with the remaining ingredients except for the paprika. Blend until the soup is creamy. Chill until ready to serve.

Serve in chilled bowls, each garnished with a sprinkling of paprika.

Yogurt Soup

1 medium onion, finely chopped
4 tablespoons butter
2 cups homemade chicken stock, strained
¼ cup pearled barley, soaked overnight
salt and pepper
2 tablespoons finely chopped parsley
1 egg
2 cups plain yogurt
juice of ½ lemon (optional)
2 tablespoons dried mint, crushed

SERVES 4

Sauté the onion in the butter until soft and golden. Add the chicken stock and simmer until just below boiling point. Add the drained barley and cook until tender, about 20 minutes. Add the seasoning and parsley.

Beat the egg lightly, add it to the yogurt and blend together well. Then add a little warm stock to the yogurt and mix. Pour the yogurt slowly into the stock, and stir over low heat – do not boil or the yogurt will curdle – for 10 to 15 minutes. A few drops of fresh lemon juice add zest to this delicious soup. Garnish with the mint.

PAGES 46 AND 47
Chilled cucumber and yogurt soup (top left) is ideal for a summer's day. Thick and creamy Carrot soup (top right) is delicious served chilled. The recipe for Yogurt soup has Armenian origins.

Egg and Lemon Soup

5 cups homemade chicken stock
salt and pepper, to taste
¼ cup long-grain rice
2 eggs
juice of 1 medium lemon
parsley, to garnish

SERVES 6

Heat, but do not boil, the chicken stock, then season with salt and pepper. Add the rice and simmer until it is tender, 10 to 15 minutes.

Meanwhile, prepare the sauce. Beat the eggs in a small bowl, gradually adding the lemon juice at the same time.

When ready to serve, slowly add the lemon juice mixture to the soup, which should be hot but not boiling (the eggs will curdle if it does boil). Leave to stand for a few minutes, then garnish with fresh parsley and serve.

Fish Soup

2 medium onions, chopped

2 cloves garlic, crushed

4 tablespoons olive oil

2 pounds white fish

1 small crab, cracked

1 handful mussels, beards
   removed and cleaned

1 leek, white part only, chopped

1 tablespoon cider vinegar

1 teaspoon turmeric

½ teaspoon ground allspice

salt and freshly ground black
   pepper, to taste

1 sprig each of fennel and
   savory

2 bay leaves

2 egg yolks

juice of 1 lemon

2 tablespoons finely chopped
   parsley

SERVES 6

Only fresh fish will do for this soup. First sauté the onions and garlic in a little of the olive oil. Transfer this to a deep saucepan and add everything except the egg yolks, lemon juice and parsley. Add 5½ cups water and simmer for 1½ hours until a rich broth is obtained.

Strain this broth to get a clear soup, or simply remove any bones, skin and crab and mussel shells. Some cooks put the fish in a cloth and suspend it over a bowl. The juice is then left to flow through, and then the cloth wrung out to extract every drop of flavor.

Beat the egg yolks and slowly add the lemon juice. Take a ladle of the broth and add to this mixture, stirring gently. Finally add the egg and lemon mixture to the saucepan of broth, stir well and simmer on a low heat until ready to serve.

Garnish with the parsley and grind more black pepper over the top.

Feast-day Soup

salt and freshly ground black
    pepper
1 pound finely ground lean
    lamb
1 medium onion, very finely
    chopped
pinch of ground cinnamon
¼ cup long-grain rice or
    vermicelli
2½ cups homemade beef stock
juice of 1 lemon
1 tablespoon butter
chopped parsley, to garnish
1 to 2 tablespoons tomato paste
    (optional)

SERVES ABOUT 4

Season the meat and knead it well. Add the onion and cinnamon and mix thoroughly. With moistened hands, roll the meat into marble-sized balls.

Boil the rice in some water until semi-cooked, then add the stock, meatballs, and lemon juice. Simmer together until the rice is tender, about 15 minutes. Cool.

Reheat just prior to serving, dot with the butter and sprinkle with the parsley. You can stir in a tablespoon or so of tomato paste to vary this traditional soup from Jordan, if you wish.

Lentil Soup

1 large onion, finely chopped
4 tablespoons butter
1 cup lentils, soaked overnight
    and drained
5 cups homemade beef stock
1 teaspoon ground cumin
salt and freshly ground black
    pepper
3 slices white bread, crusts
    removed, diced
1 clove garlic, crushed
2 tablespoons olive oil
3 tablespoons lemon juice
finely chopped parsley, to
    garnish

SERVES 6

Sauté the onion gently in half the butter until soft, then add the drained lentils and stir until glazed with the butter. Add the stock, cumin and salt and pepper, then simmer until the lentils have almost disintegrated, 1½ to 2 hours. Test the lentils to make sure they are tender, then let cool. Purée the cool mixture briefly in a blender or food processor.

Fry the diced bread in the remaining butter with the crushed garlic to make croutons for serving with the soup.

Return the soup to the pan, reheat and bring gently to a boil. Leave to stand for a few minutes before serving, then stir in the oil, lemon juice and croutons. Garnish with a little parsley.

From Jordan, Feast-day soup (left) is eaten on auspicious occasions. Lentil soup (top) enjoys wide popularity, especially in Egypt and the Levant – Lebanon, Syria and Jordan.

Vegetable and Beef Soup

1 large onion, finely sliced
3 tablespoons olive oil
1 pound stewing beef, cubed
1 large potato, peeled and sliced
1 red pepper, seeded and sliced
2 carrots, peeled and thinly sliced
²/₃ cup shredded white cabbage
5¹/₂ cups homemade beef stock
1 tablespoon tomato paste
1 teaspoon dill
salt and pepper
2 tablespoons tarragon vinegar
finely chopped parsley, to garnish (optional)

SERVES 6

Using a deep skillet, sauté the onion gently in the olive oil until it is soft. Add the meat, shaking the pan frequently to prevent the meat from sticking, and cook for 5 minutes. Add the vegetables and cook 10 minutes longer, turning frequently.

Transfer everything to a large, heavy-based saucepan and add the stock, tomato paste, dill and seasoning. Simmer gently on a low heat for 1 to 1½ hours.

Leave the soup to cool, then remove the fat layer from the top. Reheat just before serving, adding the vinegar as a final touch. Garnish with chopped parsley if you like.

Zucchini Soup

3½ tablespoons olive oil

1 pound zucchini, washed, dried and thinly sliced

2 cloves garlic, crushed

1 large onion, thinly sliced

2½ cups homemade chicken stock

3 tablespoons finely chopped parsley

salt and freshly ground white pepper

2 teaspoons lemon juice

SERVES 4

Heat the oil in a large saucepan, then add the zucchini, garlic and onion, and simmer for 10 to 15 minutes on low heat. Add the stock, parsley and seasoning and simmer for 15 minutes.

Leave the soup to cool. Stir in the lemon juice and then purée the soup in a blender until almost smooth. Reheat without boiling and serve immediately.

Picking lettuce in the Jordan valley. Fresh salads are a feature of Middle Eastern meals.

Salads

Some Middle Eastern countries are as much as two-thirds desert – where it may not rain for years – but revenues from oil and gas deposits, and ingenious irrigation techniques, enable even these places to cultivate vegetables.

Drip irrigation, where each plant has its own "dribble tap," means that many of the arid Persian Gulf states can grow luscious fruit and vegetables. Barren for thousands of years, the desert responds almost magically to water and fertilizers. Sustained on desalinated water, cucumbers and cabbages grow twice as big as European strains, and the regional tomato yield is prodigious.

In the Fertile Crescent, huge dams irrigate thousands of acres of previously arid countryside. In Syria, the Euphrates Dam has opened the dry eastern province of Raqqa to farming. I met Bedouin who had forsaken their nomadic existence to cultivate lettuces and other seedlings outside their tents.

In Jordan, water from the River Yarmuk is diverted through the East Ghor Canal from which feeder canals irrigate farms along the eastern bank of the River Jordan. The area harvests two crops a year, with entire families, even young children, turning out to help.

Crude farm tools in the National Museum in Baghdad attest to the early skills of Mesopotamian farmers. Iraq's largest flood control and irrigation system now centers on the Tharthar Reservoir, which irrigates the arid plains northwest of Baghdad. But the greatest dam in the Middle East is the 12,230-foot-long Aswan Dam in Egypt. The dam has made perennial irrigation possible all along the Nile Valley.

The Arab's fascination with water and his ability to utilize even the smallest amounts dates back about 3,000 years to when the ancient Egyptians built a vast dam across Wadi Gerrawi. Then, using neither mortar or mechanization, the Sabaean tribe in southern Arabia built the giant Marib Dam in what is now known as Yemen. Ancient texts say that the creation of the dam turned the district into a paradise. Strabo writes of abundant fruits and of great flocks of sheep in the meadows. The collapse of the dam inundated hundreds of miles of farmland, and today Marib has been overtaken by seas of drifting sand, with a wall and sluice gate being the only evidence of the dam's existence.

On the barren central plateau of Iran, farmers have for centuries farmed by means of ingenious subterranean canals, or *kanats*, linking the strings of wells. Similar *falaj*, or underground irrigation channels, are found in al-Buraimi Oasis on the border of Abu Dhabi and the Sultanate of Oman.

So while some countries are still far from being self-sufficient, it is incorrect to associate dates alone with the Arab world. Some of the sweetest, crispest salads I have ever eaten have been in the Middle East.

Salads like *tabbouleh* are often served as an appetizer. Otherwise, a fresh salad is invariably served with the main course.

As its name implies, *salata Arabieh* belongs to no particular country, but I always associate it with Lebanon. Char-broiled fish and barbecued *kebabs* always arrive with a bowl of chopped tomatoes, cucumbers and onions, all shiny and inviting beneath a dressing of garlic, lemon juice and olive oil.

Fattouche, a popular Syrian peasant salad, uses crumbled bread as a variation on the theme. Additional flavors can include chopped fresh mint, parsley and cilantro.

The recipe for tomato and cilantro salad in this chapter comes from Yemen, where local cooks have devised all kinds of highly original cold sauces and dips. I am equally happy with just a plain tomato and chopped onion salad, sprinkled with pepper and drenched in oil and lemon juice. White cheese, local bread and a tomato and onion salad became a favorite lunch when I was staying at the Winter Palace Hotel, overlooking the Nile at Luxor in Egypt.

The use of yogurt in salads is common in Middle Eastern cuisines, especially in Turkey and Jordan. Cucumber, nut and yogurt salad is a wonderful summer appetizer. Another Turkish dish, eggplant salad, is one of my favorites. Cooked spinach also enjoys a close affinity with yogurt, either plain or with garlic. Garlic, of course, is very much prized in the Middle East.

Olive oil, garlic and chopped fresh parsley flavor this Kidney bean salad. The recipe uses dried beans, but you can also use canned.

Kidney Bean Salad

2¹⁄₃ cups dried kidney beans
juice of 1¹⁄₂ to 2 lemons
4 tablespoons olive oil
salt and black pepper
1 green bell pepper, chopped
6 scallions, finely chopped
1 clove garlic, crushed
1 tablespoon chopped parsley, plus extra, to
    garnish

SERVES 4 to 6

Soak the beans overnight in plenty of cold water, then rinse and drain them. Boil fast for 15 minutes, then simmer for 1½ to 2 hours until tender, skimming the surface as necessary.

Prepare the dressing by mixing the lemon juice, olive oil and salt and pepper together. Pour over the beans, then mix in the green pepper, onions, garlic and parsley.

Line a bowl with lettuce leaves and tip in the bean salad. Garnish with a little more parsley.

Fattouche

1 medium cucumber
1 stale pita bread
1 cup coarsely chopped onion
4 scallions, coarsely chopped (optional)
small lettuce, shredded
4 tablespoons finely chopped parsley
4 medium tomatoes, coarsely chopped
2 tablespoons chopped fresh mint
juice of 2 large lemons
6 tablespoons olive oil
2 cloves garlic, crushed
salt and pepper, to taste

SERVES 4 to 6

Chop the cucumber, then sprinkle with salt and leave it to stand for 30 minutes. Rinse well and pat dry.

Break the bread into small pieces and put in a large mixing bowl. Add the chopped onions, scallions, lettuce, parsley, tomatoes, mint and cucumber. Mix together well.

Now make a dressing with the lemon juice, olive oil and garlic. Season with salt and black pepper and pour over the salad mixture. Toss together well and chill before serving.

Salata Arabieh

6 medium tomatoes, diced
1 large cucumber, peeled and diced
2 medium onions, finely chopped
2 cloves garlic, finely chopped
1 medium green bell pepper, seeded and diced
    (optional)
4 tablespoons chopped fresh mint
4 tablespoons finely chopped fresh parsley
juice of 1¹⁄₂ to 2 lemons
4 tablespoons olive oil
salt and freshly ground black pepper

SERVES 6

Combine all the vegetables in a bowl. Mix the remaining ingredients together and pour over the vegetables. Toss together very well and chill before serving with pita bread.

PAGES 58 AND 59 *Two traditional Middle Eastern salads that capture the flavors of the region:* Fattouche *(left) and* Salata Arabieh.

Cucumber and Raisin Salad with Yogurt

2 medium cucumbers
salt and freshly ground white
pepper
¾ cup plain yogurt
⅓ cup raisins
¼ cup chopped walnuts
2 scallions, finely chopped
pinch of ground cumin
1½ tablespoons chopped fresh
mint

SERVES 3 OR 4

Slice the cucumbers, sprinkle with salt and leave to drain in a colander for 30 minutes.
    Combine the yogurt, raisins, walnuts, scallions, cumin and salt and pepper in a bowl. Add the cucumber and mix well. Stir in the mint, then chill until ready to serve.

Eggplant Salad

3 medium eggplants
salt
6 tablespoons olive oil
3 cloves garlic, crushed
freshly ground black pepper
½ cup plain yogurt
pinch each of paprika and
cumin

SERVES 6

Cut the eggplants into ¼ inch thick slices. Sprinkle with salt and leave for 30 minutes, weighted down with a flat dish, to remove the bitter juices. Rinse the eggplant slices and pat dry on paper towels.
    Sauté the slices in very hot oil until they are crisp on both sides. Drain on paper towels.
    Mix the garlic and salt and pepper into the yogurt. Arrange the eggplant slices in layers in a flat serving dish and coat well with the yogurt. Sprinkle with the paprika and cumin and chill until ready to serve.

Spinach Salad

1 pound fresh spinach
¾ cup plain yogurt
1 clove garlic, crushed
pinch of cumin
salt and pepper

SERVES 4

Clean the fresh spinach under running water and remove the stems and any large veins. Chop the leaves and simmer in just the moisture clinging to the leaves until tender, about 20 minutes. Cool.
    Blend the yogurt with the garlic, cumin and seasonings. Add to the spinach and mix well. Chill until ready to serve.

Salads are especially popular in Turkey and Iran. This selection includes Cucumber and raisin salad with yogurt (top left), Eggplant salad (top right) and Spinach salad. Each salad is delicious served with pita bread.

Tomato and Cilantro Salad

6 firm, ripe medium tomatoes
½ bunch fresh cilantro leaves,
chopped
pinch of paprika
salt and freshly ground black
pepper
2½ tablespoons olive oil
juice of 1 lemon

SERVES 4

Scald, peel and slice the tomatoes into a bowl. Sprinkle with the chopped cilantro leaves.

Combine the paprika, salt and pepper, oil and lemon juice, and beat together vigorously. Pour over the tomatoes, then chill. Remove the salad from the refrigerator 10 minutes before serving.

Salata Fil-Fil Green pepper salad

4 medium green bell peppers
juice of 1½ to 2 lemons
4 tablespoons olive oil
dash of vinegar
1 clove garlic, crushed
salt, to taste
ripe olives, to garnish

SERVES 4

Slice or quarter the bell peppers lengthwise, then remove the seeds. Char under the broiler until the edges are brown and crisp. Leave to cool.

Make the dressing by mixing together the remaining ingredients, then pour it over the peppers. Mix well, and garnish with ripe olives.

Potato Salad

2 pounds new potatoes,
scrubbed
good pinch of cumin
4 tablespoons olive oil
juice of 1½ to 2 lemons
3 cloves garlic, crushed
salt and pepper
3 tablespoons finely chopped
scallions
4 tablespoons finely chopped
parsley

SERVES 4 to 6

Boil the potatoes until they are just tender. Leave them to cool a little, then cut them into uniform chunks. Sprinkle with cumin.

Prepare the dressing by mixing together the oil, lemon juice, garlic and salt and pepper. Pour over the potatoes. Toss well, then chill until required.

Serve sprinkled with the scallions and parsley.

The variety of produce in these salads reflects the many vegetables featured in Middle Eastern cooking. Try Salata Fil-Fil, or Green pepper salad (top left), Potato salad (middle) and Tomato and cilantro salad.

Green Bean, Leek and Asparagus Salad

*1 pound prepared vegetables
   (see method)*
*salt and freshly ground black
   pepper*
1 clove garlic, crushed
4½ tablespoons olive oil
juice of 1½ to 2 lemons

SERVES 4

This salad can be made with any variety of green beans, leeks or asparagus. Top, tail and slice the beans if large; wash and slice the leeks; scrape and trim the asparagus stems.

Cook each vegetable in a little salted water until barely tender, then drain and leave to cool.

Make a dressing by mixing together the garlic, oil and lemon juice with salt and pepper. Pour over the salad just before serving.

A merchant and his carrot mountain in the Nile delta. Carrots are just one of the colorful vegetables sold in Middle Eastern markets.

Vegetables and Rice

While the western vogue for vegetarian cooking has only recently elevated vegetables to "main course" status, vegetables have a historically important position on Middle Eastern menus. A frequently quoted saying during Abbasid times was: "A table without vegetables is like an old man devoid of wisdom."

Many dishes, such as vegetable casserole, are meals in themselves. So is stuffed eggplant, a great favorite of Abbasid society; the Caliph Wathiq was reportedly so fond of eggplants that he ate forty at a time. Iraqis transform the humble potato with a ground meat and pine nut filling, while the stuffed tomatoes of Egypt and the Levant have no equal.

Although many Middle Eastern cities today have large, western-style supermarkets, people still turn to the traditional souks for buying fresh vegetables. Store owners display an artistic bent with colorful arrangements of polished tomatoes, shiny zucchini, red and green bell peppers and purple eggplants. It is unthinkable not to be able to select your own vegetables, which are hunted down as soon as the souk opens. Usually the cook or a servant does the shopping, but in some countries it might be the grandmother with one of the servants' sons to carry her basket.

I especially remember an old Palestinian woman, possibly blind, groping slowly through the vegetable market in east Jerusalem. No doubt she knew her way and was probably a familiar figure, small, wrinkled and wearing a long, black robe. Stopping outside one store, she felt around the display, then held up a smooth-skinned eggplant, handing her purse trustingly to the owner for him to extract payment. While waiting, she popped a grape into her mouth; then, smiling like a guilty child, she continued her shopping. I watched her buying a lettuce, lemons and bundles of cilantro before losing sight of her in the crowds.

In conservative Arab states such as Qatar and Kuwait, it is common for men to do the shopping. By contrast, in Sana'a, well-veiled women sell onions, carrots, tomatoes and other vegetables coaxed from the rocky soil.

The most commonly used Middle Eastern vegetables – zucchini, bell peppers, spinach, and so on – are easily available in the United States. If you have trouble finding others, such as okra, try a Caribbean or Asian grocery store. Always buy parsley to garnish with, and never be without a lemon when cooking the Middle Eastern way.

Several recipes in this chapter are ideal for vegetarians: the popular *Imam bayıldı* (or swooning Imam), cabbage rolls, okra in oil and bean stew can make an entire buffet. Iran's contribution is an unusual combination of herbs and nuts in an omelet. Spinach is supposed to be native to Iran, but my recipe for spinach pie comes from Turkey, a delicious party dish that can be eaten hot or cold.

Wheat and rice are the main grains used in Middle Eastern cooking. Cracked wheat, or *bulghur*, is more usually encountered in ground-meat dishes, but it can be eaten plain with butter, topped with a fresh tomato paste or garlic-flavored yogurt with black pepper.

Rice is the basic dish throughout the Middle East: *roz* to the Arabs, *pilav* (cooked with other ingredients) in Turkey, and *chelo* (steamed) or *polo* (cooked with other ingredients) in Iran. Basmati rice, which resembles the high-grade southern rice, is preferred, often colored with saffron or turmeric. A common way of serving it is in a ring garnished with a sauce and nuts. Meats and fish are frequently served on a bed of rice, a good example being the Bedouin whole roast lamb. Following a visit to Iran in 1971, I encountered *chelo*, a rice so subtle that I tend to make it to this day, the exception being saffron rice to serve with fish.

Last, but vital to millions of poorer people in the Middle East, are the dishes based on dried beans and peas: *foul medames*, a bean dish, is almost the national dish of Egypt. Most bean and lentil recipes are geared to peasant tastes – chick-peas have already appeared in this book in the guise of *hummus*, and there is a recipe for lentil soup, along with lamb and chick-pea casserole in the meat chapter.

We know that Middle Eastern cooks use a great deal of yogurt. Plain, or spiked with garlic, it can be served with fried, sautéed or baked vegetables. Lemon juice is routinely used to heighten the flavor of many vegetable dishes like cabbage rolls or baked eggplant.

Batata Charp Stuffed potatoes

8 medium potatoes
1 egg
1 tablespoon cornstarch
salt and pepper
½ cup vegetable oil

Filling
1 medium onion, finely chopped
3 tablespoons butter
pinch each of paprika, ground coriander and allspice
½ pound lean ground beef

SERVES 4 to 6

First make the filling. Sauté the onion in the butter until golden and soft. Add the seasonings, then the meat and cook for about 5 minutes until the meat changes color. Remove and set aside.

Peel and boil the potatoes. Mash them well in a large bowl, then add the egg, cornstarch and salt and pepper, mixing all in very thoroughly.

With moist hands break off a lump the size of a golf ball. Roll it in your hands, then flatten it on your work surface and make a small hollow in the top. Fill this with 1 teaspoonful of the meat mixture and close the edges. Roll the potato ball around in your hands to ensure the meat is well sealed inside. Repeat this procedure until all the meat and potatoes are used up. Refrigerate the potato balls for at least 1 hour.

Heat the oil in a deep saucepan. When the oil is sizzling, gently lower a potato ball into the saucepan and cook quickly, turning on all sides until it is golden brown. Cook each ball separately and be careful it does not break. Drain well on paper towels.

This amount makes about 15 potato balls. Serve with a chopped salad, bread and a *labneh* (page 28) dip.

Stuffed Tomatoes

4 large, firm tomatoes
salt and pepper
1 onion, finely chopped
5 tablespoons olive oil
⅓ cup long-grain rice
pinch of sugar
1 tablespoon currants
1 tablespoon pine nuts, chopped
1 tablespoon finely chopped mint
1 tablespoon finely chopped parsley

SERVES 4

Select tomatoes of a uniform size. Carefully slice off the tops and set aside. Scoop out the pulp with a small spoon, removing any hard core, then chop the pulp. Sprinkle the inside of each tomato case with salt and pepper, and leave upside-down to drain on paper towels.

Sauté the onion gently in the olive oil until soft and golden. Add the tomato pulp, and the remaining ingredients, then simmer on low heat for 3 minutes. Add ⅔ cup water and cook gently until the rice softens, about 10 minutes. Meanwhile preheat the oven to 350°F.

Leave the mixture to cool, then spoon it into each tomato case, leaving enough room for the rice to swell. Top each tomato with its own "lid," and arrange side-by-side in an oiled baking dish. Brush each with a little extra oil and bake for 30 minutes.

Imam Bayildi   Baked eggplant

3 medium eggplants
salt
1 cup chopped onion
6 tablespoons olive oil
3 cloves garlic, crushed
*1 small red bell pepper, seeded
    and diced*
*3 medium tomatoes, skinned
    and finely chopped*
*2 tablespoons pine nuts,
    chopped*
*1 ½ tablespoons raisins,
    chopped*
½ teaspoon paprika
juice of 1 lemon
extra olive oil, to finish

SERVES 6

Cut the eggplants in half lengthwise. Using a spoon, scoop out the flesh, being careful not to puncture the skins. Leave a shell about ¼ inch thick. Chop and salt the pulp, place in a colander, and leave to drain for 1 hour. Rinse under cold water, then pat dry with paper towels. Rinse and dry the shells as well.

Fry the onion in some of the oil until it softens. Mix in the garlic and cook for 3 minutes longer. Stir in the eggplant pulp, the pepper and tomatoes, and cook over medium heat until the pepper softens and most of the liquid has evaporated. Remove the pan from the heat and mix in the pine nuts, raisins, paprika and salt.

Preheat the oven to 350°F, and put the remaining oil in a baking dish. Arrange the eggplant shells in it, in a close-fitting layer. Fill each shell with the stuffing and sprinkle with lemon juice.

Gently add boiling water down one side of the baking dish to come about half-way up the eggplants. Cover with foil and bake in the oven for about 1 hour. Remove the dish when the shells are tender, and leave the eggplants to cool in the sauce.

When the eggplants are cool, drain off excess liquid and trickle a little extra olive oil over the shells. Chill until about 10 minutes before serving.

Stuffed vegetables are always popular with Middle Eastern cooks. Stuffed potatoes (top left) are a favorite in Iraq. Stuffed tomatoes (top right) are delicious eaten either hot or cold. Baked eggplant, here ready for the oven, is a medieval Turkish dish that has never fallen out of favor.

Baked Eggplants with Cumin

2 pounds medium eggplants
6 cloves garlic, crushed
4 tablespoons olive oil
1 teaspoon paprika
1 heaped teaspoon ground
cumin
2 pinches cayenne pepper
salt
butter
lemon juice

SERVES 4

Preheat the oven to 450°F.

Wash and dry the eggplants. Slit the skins in several places to prevent them bursting, then steam until tender, 30 to 40 minutes (in a pressure cooker, 12 to 15 minutes). Leave to cool, then cut each eggplant into 3 strips lengthwise. Sprinkle with the garlic.

Heat the oil in a baking dish in the oven. Put in the eggplants and sprinkle with

paprika, cumin, cayenne pepper, salt and dabs of butter. Bake for 5 minutes.

Just before serving, sprinkle with a few drops of fresh lemon juice.

Cabbage Rolls

½ cup long-grain rice

3 tablespoons olive oil

2 medium onions, finely chopped

2 cloves garlic, crushed

2 tablespoons pine nuts, chopped

pinch each of ground cumin, ground allspice and paprika

½ pound finely ground lamb

1 tablespoon dried mint

salt

12 large cabbage leaves

lemon juice (optional)

2 medium tomatoes, skinned and chopped (optional)

cream (optional)

SERVES 6

Cook the rice as for Plain *pilav* rice (page 78).

To make the stuffing, heat the oil in a large skillet and sauté the onions, garlic and pine nuts with the spices until golden. Add the lamb and mint with a pinch of salt and cook lightly, turning frequently in the pan. Meanwhile, preheat the oven to 350°F.

Make sure you use large, whole cabbage leaves. Plunge the leaves into boiling, salted water to make them pliable, then spread them out on a wooden board and cut out the cores. Place a portion of stuffing on each leaf and roll up into a neat package, folding up the end and folding in the sides.

Arrange the cabbage rolls close together in a shallow, greased baking dish and add slightly salted water to almost cover. Make sure they are tightly packed or they might unwrap while cooking.

Cover and cook for 30 minutes, or until the leaves are tender. Serve hot sprinkled with lemon juice, or with a sauce made from tomatoes and cream puréed together.

Green Bean Stew

2 pounds green beans

Tomato sauce
3 cloves garlic, crushed
½ teaspoon ground coriander
2 tablespoons olive oil
2 medium onions, chopped
1½ tablespoons tomato paste
6 medium tomatoes, skinned
1 tablespoon chopped parsley
salt and white pepper
½ teaspoon paprika
juice of 1 lemon

SERVES 6

First, prepare the tomato sauce. Sauté the garlic and coriander in the oil, then add the onions and cook the mixture for 10 minutes, stirring occasionally. Add the tomato paste, tomatoes and parsley and crush and blend into a purée. Mix in the salt, pepper, paprika and lemon juice and simmer, uncovered, for 15 minutes. Stir frequently to make a rich, aromatic sauce.

Top and tail the beans, then place them in a large saucepan with the sauce and enough water to barely cover. Simmer until tender, about 15 minutes.

If you prefer your beans *al dente*, remove them after 10 minutes and set aside while you reduce the sauce to a thicker consistency. Return the beans to the sauce and reheat to serve.

Zucchini with Tomatoes

2 pounds zucchini
2 cloves garlic, crushed
pinch of ground coriander
3 tablespoons olive oil
6 medium tomatoes, skinned
*   and chopped*
salt and black pepper
1½ tablespoons chopped
*   parsley*
½ cup lemon juice

SERVES 4

Wash and dry the zucchini, then slice them fairly thickly.

Sauté the garlic and coriander in the oil, then add the zucchini slices. Cook gently for about 15 minutes, turning frequently.

Add the tomatoes, salt and pepper, parsley, lemon juice and ½ cup water. Simmer until tender, about 20 minutes. Serve hot.

Okra Stew

6 medium tomatoes, sliced
1 pound fresh okra
cider vinegar
3 cloves garlic, crushed
2 medium onions, finely
    chopped
1 teaspoon ground coriander

3 tablespoons olive oil
salt and pepper
1 tablespoon tomato paste
ground cumin
juice of 1 lemon

SERVES 4

Scald, skin and slice the tomatoes. Wash and cut off the okra stems, taking care not to puncture the pods. Soak the okra in vinegar for 30 minutes to prevent them from becoming sticky during cooking. Drain and rinse well.

Sauté the garlic, onions and coriander in the olive oil until soft. Add the okra and cook gently for 5 to 10 minutes, stirring occasionally.

Place half the okra mixture in a greased flameproof casserole and cover with a layer of sliced tomatoes. Make another layer of onion and okra and arrange more tomatoes on top. Season with salt and pepper and top with the remaining tomatoes.

Mix the tomato paste with a little water and pour over the vegetables, then add enough water to almost cover the top layer of tomatoes. Add a good pinch of cumin. Simmer over medium heat about 10 minutes. Meanwhile, preheat the oven to 350°F.

Remove the casserole from the heat, add lemon juice and bake in oven until the okra are quite tender, 30 to 40 minutes. Serve hot straight from the casserole.

Slow, gentle cooking brings out the flavors of these vegetable dishes: Green bean stew (below left); Okra stew (top right), and Zucchini with tomatoes.

Herb and Nut Omelet

3 tablespoons butter
6 scallions, finely chopped
2 lettuce leaves, finely chopped
1 teaspoon dried dill, or 2½
    tablespoons fresh dill
4 tablespoons chopped parsley
8 eggs
saffron, or ¼ teaspoon
    turmeric, to color
pinch of ground cinnamon
salt and pepper
pinch of baking soda
¼ cup chopped walnuts
2 tablespoons raisins, roughly
    chopped (optional)

SERVES 4

Melt half the butter in a skillet with an ovenproof handle. Add the scallions, lettuce, dill and parsley and sauté until the scallions are transparent. Add the remaining butter and leave to melt.

Preheat the oven to 350°F.

Beat the eggs well, then add saffron or turmeric, cinnamon, salt and pepper and baking soda. Stir in the nuts, and the raisins, if you are using them. Pour this mixture into the skillet but do not stir. Transfer to the preheated oven and bake until golden and set.

Serve immediately, either on its own or with a tomato salad.

Baked Squash in Tahini Sauce

4 medium yellow squash

½ cup butter

3 medium onions, finely chopped

4 cloves garlic, crushed

pepper

½ teaspoon ground coriander

½ teaspoon paprika

¼ teaspoon ground cinnamon

1 pound lean ground lamb or beef

salt

4 tablespoons tahini *(sesame seed paste)*

5 tablespoons lemon juice, or more, to taste

SERVES 4 to 6

Preheat the oven to 375°F. Peel the squash and cut it into slices about ½ inch thick. Sauté the squash the butter until almost cooked and golden. Set aside.

In the same pan, sauté the onions and half of the crushed garlic. Season with pepper, coriander, paprika and cinnamon, then add the meat and cook until lightly brown. Add salt.

Line a greased baking dish with a layer of closely packed squash, spread the meat mixture over it and then layer with remaining squash.

Blend together the *tahini*, lemon juice, remaining garlic and salt to taste in a bowl. Blend to the consistency of paste, adding more lemon juice if necessary. Pour

this into the casserole and bake until the top turns a golden brown, about 40 minutes.

Turkish Vegetable Casserole

1 medium eggplant, sliced
salt
4 medium okra, each about
   3 inches long
2 medium onions, chopped
5 to 7 tablespoons olive oil
1 green bell pepper, seeded and
   chopped
4 medium zucchini, unpeeled
   and coarsely chopped
1 cup chopped green beans
1/2 cup shelled peas
2 1/2 cups peeled and cubed
   potatoes
4 cloves garlic, crushed
1 bunch of parsley, finely
   chopped
2 teaspoons paprika
1 heaped teaspoon ground
   cumin
1 1/2 cups chicken or vegetable
   stock
5 to 6 medium tomatoes,
   skinned and sliced
1 teaspoon sugar

SERVES 6 to 8

Soak the eggplant slices in salted water for 30 minutes, then remove and drain well. Prepare okra as for Okra stew (page 73). Preheat the oven to 375°F.

Sauté the onions in a little of the oil until soft and golden. Transfer to a casserole and add the remaining vegetables, except the tomatoes. Add the garlic, parsley, all the seasonings, stock and most of the olive oil. Mix together, then add the tomatoes and dribble in the remaining olive oil. Flatten the vegetables with a wooden spoon.

Cover and bake for about 1 hour, or until the vegetables are tender. Remove the casserole from the oven, add salt to taste and the sugar, then stir well and cook for 15 to 20 minutes longer. Serve the vegetable casserole with bread as a hot dip.

The Turks calls this dish *turlu guvec*, and they like to serve it cold.

Spinach Pie

*1 pound phyllo pastry, thawed if
    frozen*
1¼ cups olive oil

Filling
*2½ pounds spinach, thawed if
    frozen*
salt and pepper
2 medium onions, chopped
1½ tablespoons butter
4 large eggs, beaten
1 cup milk, warmed
*½ pound feta cheese, crumbled,
    or Parmesan and feta
    cheeses, mixed*
2 teaspoon dried dill
1 heaped teaspoon paprika

SERVES 6 to 8

First prepare the filling. If using fresh spinach, wash it, remove the stems and any large veins and cut the leaves into thin strips. Sprinkle with salt and leave for 1 hour. Then rub the leaves and squeeze out all the liquid. Follow package directions if using frozen spinach.

Sauté the onions in the butter until transparent. Beat the eggs in a bowl. Blend in the warm milk and add the onions, cheese, dill and paprika. Mix well with the spinach. Add salt and pepper to taste.

Preheat the oven to 350°F. Grease a 10- x 12-inch baking dish.

Brush one side of one sheet of the pastry dough with oil and lay it in the dish,

which it will overlap. Brush 5 more sheets individually with oil and place them on top. Now add the spinach filling on this and trickle 2 tablespoons olive oil over it.

Bring the overlapping dough up over the filling. Cut the last 6 sheets to the size of the dish, brush them individually with oil and lay them on top.

Score the top into squares and sprinkle with water to prevent the edges curling. Bake until the top is golden brown, 30 to 45 minutes. Leave to set before cutting.

Saffron Rice

2 cups long-grain rice
salt
3 tablespoons pine nuts
2 medium onions, finely
  chopped
2 tablespoons olive oil
2 tablespoons raisins
saffron, or ½ teaspoon tumeric,
  for color

SERVES 4

Boil the rice in a saucepan of salted water briskly for 2 to 3 minutes. Remove from heat and rinse through a strainer until the water is clear. Set aside to drain.

Sauté the pine nuts and onions in the oil. Add the raisins and the rice, stirring gently for 1 to 2 minutes, until the rice grains are well coated.

Return the rice mixture to a saucepan, add the saffron or tumeric, a pinch of salt and enough water to come 1 inch above the surface. Stir, then leave the rice to simmer gently, uncovered, until all the water is absorbed. Set aside 10 minutes before stirring and serving.

Chelo   Persian steamed rice

2 cups long-grain rice
salt
¼ cup butter, melted
4 egg yolks (optional)

SERVES 4

Put the rice and salt in a saucepan and boil briskly for 12 to 13 minutes. The rice should be soft, but not quite done. Rinse under cold running water, until the water is clear, then set aside to drain.

Pour half the melted butter mixed with a little water into a saucepan with a thick base. Add the rice, smoothing it out.

Fold a clean dish towel in half and place it over the top of the saucepan, then cover with a lid. The towel will absorb the steam, helping the rice to remain fluffy with each grain separate. The bottom should be crisp – ensure it does not burn from being on a too high heat. Cook for about 15 minutes. Trickle the remaining butter over the rice and serve. The Persian way to serve this is to pop an egg yolk in a hollow made in each portion of the *chelo*.

Plain Pilav Rice

2 cups long-grain rice
salt
2 tablespoons olive oil

SERVES 4

Put rice and salt in a saucepan of water and boil briskly for 2 to 3 minutes. Remove from heat and rinse through a strainer under cold running water until the water is clear. Set aside to drain.

Return the rice to a saucepan, add a small pinch of salt and the olive oil. Cover with cold water to come 1 inch above the rice, then stir. Simmer, uncovered, until all the water is absorbed and small steam holes appear on the surface of the rice, about 15 minutes. Do not stir during the cooking time. Set aside for 5 to 10 minutes before serving.

Rice is a staple ingredient served throughout the Middle East, and these recipes reflect the varied ways it is prepared. Plain pilav rice (top); Chelo, or Persian steamed rice (middle), and Saffron rice, delicious for serving with seafood.

The peoples of the Gulf States are big seafood-eaters, taking advantage of the abundant selection of fish in coastal waters. Here is a fisherman with part of his day's catch in Dhofar, along the Arabian Sea coast of Oman.

Seafood

Some of my most memorable meals in the Middle East have been seafood – but then I love fish. The setting of many seafood restaurants is also a bonus. How could I forget grilled fish by the creaking waterwheels on the Orontes river in Hama, in Syria?

There is a restaurant near the Roman city of Jerash, in Jordan, that serves wonderful grilled perch – known locally as St. Peter's fish – from the Sea of Galilee. More rustic is a restaurant in Aqaba with *al fresco* tables under half a dozen straggly palms. The fish is good – you choose your own in the kitchen – but the smell of the charcoal grill attracts Aqaba's 100,000 cats, who practically drag it off your table.

Baghdad is famous for open-air restaurants serving *mashgouf*, or smoked fish, along the banks of the Tigris. The Iraqis do interesting things with fish, especially in the delta port of Basra, but some of the best seafood dishes are found in the Persian Gulf. Despite oil spills, the lukewarm waters of the Gulf abound in seafood: fish, crab, giant shrimp and a delicately flavored, flat-chested cousin of the lobster known as *umm robien*.

The early-morning fish markets of Manama, capital of Bahrain, and in Kuwait, Dubai and the other Gulf states are a hive of activity the moment the *dhows* unload. In Omani towns on the Arabian Sea, sardines and other small fish are sold straight out of the small fishing boats, or *houris*.

The Red Sea off Yemen and Saudi Arabia is equally rich in fish: barracuda, bass, cod, lobster and crabs. While the *Quran* imposes no dietary restrictions, shellfish are avoided by many Muslims, a parallel with Judaic dietary laws that forbid eating any fish without fins or scales.

And while the Mediterranean lapping southern Europe grows more toxic every day, the Eastern Mediterranean and the Aegean supply Turkey, Syria and Lebanon with a veritable treasure trove of seafood. One of the many delights of Istanbul is lunch in a sunny seafood restaurant beneath the Galatea Bridge linking the European and Asian sides of the city. At night, seafood restaurants along the Bosphorus are packed.

The world's finest caviar comes from the Caspian Sea in northern Iran. The sturgeon are netted as they congregate to spawn, and the eggs are scooped from the living fish. During my travels around the Caspian Sea, I ate beluga caviar daily for lunch, with a raw onion, lemon, salty butter and local bread. Then back in Tehran, I enjoyed beluga caviar with sour cream and *blinis*.

The most popular fish in the Middle East are red mullet (known by the grand title of *Sultan Ibrahim* in Arabic), *arous*, a fish like the French *daurade* or sea bream, and sole, sea bass, tuna and turbot.

Among freshwater fish, the *chaboute* (similar to a trout) is netted in the Tigris-Euphrates river systems in Iraq. This is the famous *mashgouf* which is cleaned, split, staked and smoked over an open fire. Pungent and tender, it is impossible to copy in a kitchen. In Basra, fish baked in date purée is popular.

Tuna and swordfish *kebabs* are a specialty of Turkey, where coastal restaurants also serve stuffed mussels and squid. *Samak mashi*, or stuffed fish, fish baked in *tahini* sauce, and baked fish eaten with *muhammara* are common in Syria and Lebanon. Arabs eat basically the same fish dishes, although an Indian influence has made seafood curries equally popular. Nile fish tend to taste muddy, but there are good seafood restaurants in Suez and Alexandria, with *saadiyeh*, or plain fish and rice, and grilled or fried small fish being common dishes.

Some Middle Eastern countries still enjoy traditional dried, salted fish. A common sight in Dhofar, in southern Oman, are sheets of silver sardines, drying along the beaches.

Wasif, tiny fish like sprats, are salted and dried by fishermen on the Tihama coast of Yemen. Trucked to the mountain towns, they are sold by the basketful in local souks. The fish adds zest to *zahawiq*, a popular Yemeni dip made from tomatoes and chilies.

Plenty of olive oil, lemon juice, and cumin are essential for cooking fish the Middle Eastern way. Grape leaves, or silver foil as a substitute, are also used for grilling, broiling and baking. Skewers are needed for fish *kebabs*, and a fish clamp will prevent large, whole fish from breaking when you turn them in the oven.

Cold Fish in Olive Oil

1 × 2-pound whole fish, such as cod, bass, mackerel or similar, gutted

6 tablespoons olive oil

1 large green bell pepper, seeded and finely chopped

2 medium onions, sliced

3 cloves garlic, crushed

6 medium tomatoes, peeled and sliced

1 tablespoon tomato paste

a bunch of parsley, finely chopped

salt and pepper

6 green and 6 ripe olives, to garnish

SERVES 4

Wash the fish and scrape off any loose scales if necessary, then pat dry on paper towels. If the skin is thick, make several diagonal slits to aid cooking. Heat the oil in a large pan and fry the fish slowly, cooking lightly on both sides for about 10 minutes. Lift it out gently, drain on paper towels and leave to cool.

Sauté the bell pepper in the same oil, then add the onions after 10 minutes and cook until both are soft. Add the garlic and sauté for 2 minutes longer. Pulp the tomatoes and blend with the paste and parsley. Add the mixture to the pan, season to taste, stir well and simmer for 15 minutes.

Lift the fish carefully back into the pan, cover with the sauce and cook gently for

10 to 15 minutes, or until tender. If the sauce is too thick, add a little water mixed with lemon juice.

Finally, remove the fish onto a large serving dish and pour the sauce over it. Garnish it with the olives, leave it to cool and then refrigerate. Remove about 10 minutes before eating.

Shrimp Curry

8 to 10 unshelled jumbo shrimp
2 tablespoons olive oil
juice of 1 large lemon
salt and black pepper
3 medium onions, sliced
1 bay leaf
1 celery stick
2 cloves garlic, crushed
1 ½ tablespoons clarified butter
1-inch piece fresh ginger root,
  peeled and grated
1 level teaspoon turmeric
1 teaspoon ground coriander
½ teaspoon ground cumin
½ teaspoon chili powder
1 heaped tablespoon shredded
  coconut
4 medium tomatoes, skinned
  and chopped
finely chopped cilantro leaves

SERVES 4

First prepare the shrimp: remove the shells and heads, then marinate the flesh in olive oil and some of the lemon juice with seasoning for 2 hours.

Put the shells in a pan, cover with cold water, add 3 slices onion, a bay leaf, celery stick and salt and pepper. Simmer until you have a rich, aromatic stock. Strain well and set aside.

In a large saucepan, sauté the garlic and remaining onion in the clarified butter until soft and transparent. Add the spices and coconut and sizzle for 1 minute.

Now add the tomatoes and remaining lemon juice and cook for 10 minutes, stirring well. Stir in the stock, marinade and shrimp, and simmer, uncovered, until the shrimp are tender and the sauce is reduced, 15 to 20 minutes.

Garnish with finely chopped cilantro leaves and serve with *pilav* rice (page 78).

This recipe is based on a popular dish made from umm robien, *a type of lobster found in the Persian Gulf. It can be adapted to crayfish or other shellfish.*

Fried Fish

*12 small fish, such as fresh
    sardines or herring*
2 cloves garlic, finely chopped
½ teaspoon ground cumin
salt and white pepper
*1½ tablespoons finely chopped
    parsley*
flour, to coat
cooking oil
*sliced lemon and tomato, to
    garnish*

SERVES 4

Wash and clean the fish under running water, then pat dry on paper towels.

Mix the garlic, cumin, salt and pepper and parsley together, then rub over the fish inside and out. Cover and chill for 1 hour so the fish absorbs the flavors.

Now roll each fish in the flour. Heat enough oil in a skillet to shallow-fry the fish. When the oil is sizzling hot, slip each fish in and cook quickly on both sides, about 10 minutes. Serve garnished with lemon and tomato.

Shrimp in Tomato Sauce

2 pounds shelled shrimp
1/2 teaspoon ground cinnamon
salt and freshly ground pepper
3 cloves garlic, crushed
2 medium onions, finely
*   chopped*
1 1/2 tablespoons oil
3 tablespoons tomato paste
5 medium tomatoes, skinned,
*   chopped and puréed*
3 tablespoons lemon juice
freshly chopped parsley

SERVES 4

Season the shrimp with cinnamon and salt and pepper.

Sauté the garlic and onions in the oil until they are soft. Blend in the tomato paste diluted with a little water and the tomatoes, stirring well. Leave to simmer over gentle heat, about 12 minutes.

Add the shrimp and cook over medium-high heat for about 10 minutes. Stir frequently and remove from heat when the shrimp are tender. Sprinkle with lemon juice and parsley. Serve on a bed of plain rice.

Baked Fish with Saffron Rice

*1 large whole fish, such as sea
    bass or sea bream, weighing
    about 4 pounds, gutted*

*2 cloves garlic, very finely
    chopped*

olive oil

3 tablespoons fresh lemon juice

salt and pepper

1 large tomato, sliced

1 lemon, sliced

*1 quantity Saffron Rice (page
    78)*

*lemon wedges and parsley, to
    garnish*

SERVES 4

Rinse and clean the fish under running water, then pat it dry with paper towels.

Rub the fish inside and out with a mixture of garlic, oil, lemon juice and salt and pepper. Place the tomato and lemon slices inside the fish and sew up with thread or use skewers. Chill for 2 hours. Meanwhile, preheat the oven to 375°F.

Place the fish in a large, greased baking dish and bake for 40 to 50 minutes until the flesh is tender and the skin is golden brown. Meanwhile, prepare the rice.

Serve on a bed of saffron rice and garnish with lemon wedges and parsley.

Barbecued Fish with Dates

¹/₂ pound pitted, dried dates

*4 whole white fish, about
    12 ounces each*

salt and pepper

*2 medium onions, finely
    chopped*

1 clove garlic, crushed

¹/₂ teaspoon turmeric

*generous pinch each of ground
    cumin, coriander,
    cardamom, nutmeg and
    cloves*

SERVES 4

Soak the dates in cold water until they become soft, about 4 hours. Gut and rinse the fish well under running water. Do not scale. Dry the cavities with paper towels, then sprinkle with a little salt and pepper.

Mix together the onion, garlic and spices with a little water, then stuff each fish with this mixture, sewing up the cavities or closing them with skewers.

Drain the dates, then purée in a food processor or blender with a little water, or push them through a strainer. Blend just

long enough to obtain a soft paste, then smear this on both sides of each fish. Cook over a barbecue for about 5 minutes on each side. Test with a fork to make sure the flesh is tender.

Serve hot with a rice dish. The skin together with the scales can be peeled off when eating. The date purée gives the flesh a pleasant, nutty flavor.

Fish in Hot Sauce

4 cloves garlic, chopped
1 1/2 teaspoons ground
   coriander
4 thick fillets white fish, about
   1/2 pound each
1 1/2 tablespoons olive oil
1 tablespoon lemon juice
salt and ground white pepper
lemon slices, garnish

Sauce
1/4 cup butter
1/2 small red bell pepper, seeded
   and diced
4 medium tomatoes, skinned
   and chopped
1 large onion, diced
1 teaspoon paprika
1/2 teaspoon ground ginger
pinch of salt and pepper
1 tablespoon tomato paste
   mixed with a little water

SERVES 4

Pound the garlic and coriander together in a mortar and pestle. Rub this into the fish fillets, then chill them, in a covered bowl for 2 hours.

Meanwhile, preheat the oven to 375°F.

Remove the fish from the bowl and rub each fillet with a mixture of the oil, lemon juice and salt and pepper. Lay the fillets in a greased baking dish, cover tightly with foil and bake for 20 to 30 minutes, until the flesh is tender and flakes easily.

Meanwhile, prepare the sauce. Melt the butter in a pan and sauté the pepper, tomatoes and onion until soft. Add the

seasonings and the tomato paste and mix together well. Simmer for 10 to 15 minutes over low heat. Transfer the fish to a serving dish and garnish with the hot sauce and lemon slices.

In the Levant, fish fillets or whole fish are baked and eaten with *muhammara* (page 30) as a side dip. Some people even spread it over their fish.

Baked Fish in Tahini Sauce

*1 whole white fish, weighing
about 2½ pounds*
juice of 2 large lemons
salt and pepper
6 tablespoons olive oil
1 large onion, chopped
6 tablespoons tahini *(sesame
seed paste)*
parsley, to garnish

SERVES 4

Preheat the oven to 400°F. Gut, scale and clean the fish under running water. Dry it and sprinkle with some of the lemon juice, then chill it for 2 hours.

Bring it to room temperature, then rub it with salt and pepper and some of the oil. Bake for 20 minutes, or until it is tender and the flesh flakes easily. While the fish is cooking, sauté the onion in the remaining oil.

Meanwhile, blend the *tahini* and remaining lemon juice together, adding water to achieve a creamy sauce. Remove the fish from the oven, sprinkle with the onions and coat with *tahini* sauce. Return to the oven and bake for 10 minutes longer. Garnish with parsley. Serve with rice and a salad.

Tuna Shashlik

1 pound fresh tuna
2 lemons
10 bay leaves
3 tablespoons olive oil
salt and black pepper
8 cherry tomatoes
bunch of fresh thyme
6 pearl onions

SERVES 4

Skin and bone the tuna, then cut it into chunks. Put it into a bowl with the juice of 1 lemon, the bay leaves and the oil. Grind black pepper over it, mix well and marinate for 1 hour, stirring frequently.

Meanwhile, wash the tomatoes. Make a small incision in each top and squeeze out the seeds. Insert a drop of oil, salt and a few thyme leaves into each tomato.

Slice the second lemon. Thread the fish, the onions, tomatoes, bay leaves and lemon slices alternately onto skewers. Pour the remaining marinade over them and season with salt and pepper.

Cook under a preheated, hot broiler for about 10 minutes. Serve immediately with *pilav* rice (page 78) and a green salad.

Stuffed Squid

6 medium squid bodies about
    6 inches long

5 tablespoons olive oil

2 medium tomatoes, skinned
    and pulped

salt and pepper

pinch of paprika

juice of 1 lemon

Stuffing

2 medium onions, finely
    chopped

3 tablespoons olive oil

⅓ cup long-grain rice

1 tablespoon finely chopped dill
    or mint

2 tablespoons finely chopped
    parsley

1 tablespoon pine nuts

a pinch of ground cumin

SERVES 4 as a main course

To clean a squid, hold the body in one hand and gently pull off the head and tentacles: the innards and clear "quill" should come away as well. Clean the body thoroughly under cold running water, discarding anything left inside. Rub off any membrane from the body and set aside. Repeat with all the squid. Chop off the tentacles and set aside for the stuffing. Discard the heads.

In a glass bowl, mix together the olive oil, the tomato pulp, salt and pepper and paprika. Place the squid bodies in this mixture, coat well and leave to marinate while you make the stuffing.

In a large pan, sauté the onions in the oil until soft. Add the chopped tentacles and cook with the onion until they change color. Add the rice, dill or mint, parsley, pine nuts and cumin, and cook 5 to 10

minutes, stirring with a wooden spoon. Leave to cool. Preheat the oven to 400°F.

Remove the squid from the marinade and partly fill each one with some of the stuffing. Leave room for the rice to swell during cooking. Secure the opening of each body with toothpicks or thread.

Arrange the squid in a lightly greased baking dish and pour over the marinade, the lemon juice and enough boiling water to almost cover them. Bake for about 50 minutes until tender. Remove and leave to cool. Serve chilled.

A familiar sight throughout the Middle East is slowly turning spitted lamb, or shawarma. The meat is often carved into a pocket of pita bread filled with salad ingredients.

Meat

My first taste of Middle Eastern cooking came in Aden, the port town on the south coast of Yemen. In 1963, a passenger liner bearing me and several hundred other young Australians called at Aden on her three-and-a-half-week voyage to Europe.

Tired of shipboard food, we streamed ashore in search of something fresh, when the aroma of grilling meat drew me into a small restaurant. Surrounded by curious men, I had my first taste of *kebabs*, and, while I have subsequently eaten them from Casablanca to Peshawar, I still remember this simple dish and the cook polishing my knife and fork on his apron.

Shish kebab, to use the full name, is credited with being a Turkish creation. The story goes that Turkish soldiers, obliged to pitch camp during the Ottoman conquests, adopted the habit of cooking skewered meat – goat, lamb, gazelle and so on – over an open fire outside their tents. In fact, it could just as easily have been devised by invading Persian or Mongol tribes.

On the subject of *kebabs*, the most important considerations are to purchase a good cut of meat and to marinate it for at least three to four hours. I usually mix a marinade made from the juice of two large onions, six tablespoons olive oil, a teaspoon of oregano, a pinch of cayenne pepper, plus salt and freshly ground black pepper, and then refrigerate the meat in the mixture overnight in a covered nonmetallic bowl. When barbecuing *kebabs*, or any other meat, fish or poultry, wait until the charcoal has ceased smoking before you start cooking. If using a broiler, cook the food quickly under high heat to seal in the juices and brown the outside. The cooking time will depend on how well-done you like your meat.

The ways of cooking meat in the Middle East are basically the same as in the West: grilling or broiling, stewing and roasting. Ground meat dishes are very popular in the Levant and Syria in particular, where women vie with each other to produce the finest *kibbeh*.

The Arabs tend to eat more barbecued meats, such as *kebabs* and lamb roasted on a spit. *Yaknéh*, or meat and vegetable stews, are common in the Levant. The Yemenis, too, are fond of stews, a popular ingredient being okra; okra *(bamieh)* is also a traditional dish in Egypt. Some Middle Eastern stews have an earthy, rather peasant-style character – like the lamb and chick-pea casserole in this chapter. The more refined Persian taste, which permeates all types of local cooking, is found in the veal and prune casserole dish, a fascinating blend of sweet-and-sour ingredients.

Stews are normally simmered for a long time on the stove. Alternatively, if the ingredients have been sealed by frying or sautéeing, they are baked in the oven.

Although often discarded in the West, bones are prized for their marrow, and a cracked bone is often added to stews for extra richness. Unlike meat for broiling or grilling, you can buy cheaper cuts for a stew. Searing meats in oil or butter traps the juices and adds a richer color to the dish. Simmering the meat, as in many Persian recipes, makes for a light, almost insipid looking stew, which is then enriched with spices, nuts and fruits. Most Middle Eastern cooks find it difficult to be precise about quantities; they tend to cook by heart with constant tastings and adjustings.

Organs are revered as we have seen with brains, liver and testicles in the chapter on *mezze*. I have marvelous memories of brains served in the Oriental buffet at the Hilton Hotel in al-Ain, the large oasis town in inland Abu Dhabi. I have eaten kidneys just about everywhere. Up early to photograph Shibam, a mountain town outside Sana'a, my driver and I had liver for breakfast. Served with a bowl of *foul* and flat whole-wheat bread, it is a specialty of Yemeni mountain towns on market day.

Lamb or mutton is the most commonly used meat throughout the Middle East. Goat is also eaten by the Bedouin, and I once came upon a wedding in Abu Dhabi where a young camel had been slain and was cooking in an enormous pot of stew.

The roast, stuffed neck of lamb makes a nice change from traditional roasted Sunday lunch. Either a leg or a shoulder can be used for *kharouf bi limoun*, but I prefer a shoulder since the meat tends to be more tender. I have cooked this time and time again with unfailingly excellent results. Easily prepared, it is also a good choice if expecting guests on a weeknight. I serve it with boiled new potatoes liberally sprinkled with cumin, and either cold bean salad or a crisp green salad.

Of the other recipes in this chapter, the okra and lamb stew recipe comes from Jordan; lamb and chick-pea casserole is found throughout the Middle East (especially in Egypt when people can afford the meat); Syrian meatloaf is a useful dish – eat it hot first, then serve it cold with a salad; and I often cook Lady's Thighs to serve as finger food at a cocktail party. They can be made before the guests arrive and kept warm in the oven.

Levantine Lamb Stew

4 tablespoons olive oil
2 cloves garlic, crushed
1 teaspoon ground coriander
*small piece of fresh ginger root,
    peeled and grated*
2 pounds lamb, cubed
2 medium onions, sliced
1/2 large lemon, cut into four
pinch of saffron or turmeric
salt and pepper, to taste
1/2 cup green olives
1/2 cup thick yogurt (optional)

SERVES 4

Heat the oil in a flameproof casserole and add the garlic, coriander, ginger and the lamb. Stir the meat in well until it is seared. Add the onions, lemon, saffron or turmeric, salt and pepper and enough water to cover all the lamb.

Bring to a boil, then reduce the heat and simmer until the lamb is tender, about 2 hours. Keep the pan covered during this time but stir the contents occasionally.

To thicken the sauce, remove the meat and leave the sauce to simmer uncovered. Strain, then stir in the olives. Stir until the sauce is as thick as you like, then return the meat to the casserole and serve.

The optional addition of yogurt makes this dish even more delicious. Just before serving, stir in the yogurt and simmer, but do not boil.

Persian Casserole with Prunes

24 prunes
juice of 3 lemons
½ cup olive oil
1 teaspoon ground coriander
salt and pepper, to taste
3 pounds veal, cut into cubes
3 tablespoons slivered almonds
¼ cup butter
2 medium onions, chopped
4½ cups stock
1½ tablespoons confectioners'
*   sugar*

SERVES ABOUT 6

Soak the prunes overnight.

The next day, prepare a marinade using half the lemon juice, the oil, the coriander and salt and pepper. Add the meat and leave to marinate, turning once, about 2 hours. Meanwhile, preheat the oven to 350°F.

While the veal is marinating, toast the almonds on a baking sheet until they turn golden.

Melt the butter in a heavy-based pan and sauté the onions until soft. Drain the veal, then add it to the pan and sear on all sides.

Add the stock, cover and simmer over gentle heat until tender.

Drain and pit the prunes, reserving about 1¼ cups of the soaking liquid. Mix in the confectioners' sugar and transfer to a new pan, then simmer gently for 10 to 15 minutes. Add the prune mixture, half the almonds and the remaining lemon juice to the veal. Stir well and simmer for 10 minutes longer.

Just before serving, sprinkle the remaining almonds on the top. Serve the casserole with a green salad and rice.

Roast Stuffed Neck of Lamb

2¹/₄ to 3 pounds boned neck of
    lamb
juice of 2 medium onions
1 tablespoon ground coriander
1 teaspoon ground ginger
salt and freshly ground black
    pepper
2 tablespoons oil

Stuffing
2¹/₄ cups long-grain rice
saffron or ¹/₂ teaspoon turmeric,
    to color
2 onions, chopped
¹/₂ cup pine nuts or blanched
    almonds
¹/₂ teaspoon ground allspice
¹/₄ cup butter
¹/₂ cup golden raisins
salt and black pepper

SERVES 4 to 6

Wipe the inside and outside of the neck with a cloth, then rub well with onion juice, coriander, ginger and salt and pepper. Set aside.

To prepare the stuffing, cook the rice until it is light and fluffy. Sauté the onions, pine nuts and allspice in the butter, then mix with the rice. Add the golden raisins, stir well and season with salt and pepper. Leave to cool.

Preheat the oven to 425°F.

Spoon the stuffing onto the lamb and roll up. Tie with string. Rub with 1 tablespoon of the oil and sear in the remaining oil in the oven.

Cook for 15 minutes, turning on all sides, then reduce the oven temperature to 375°F. Roast the meat at this heat, turn once again, then leave to become crisp. As for other lamb dishes, cooking time will depend on how well done you like your meat. Allow 30 minutes per ¹/₂ pound.

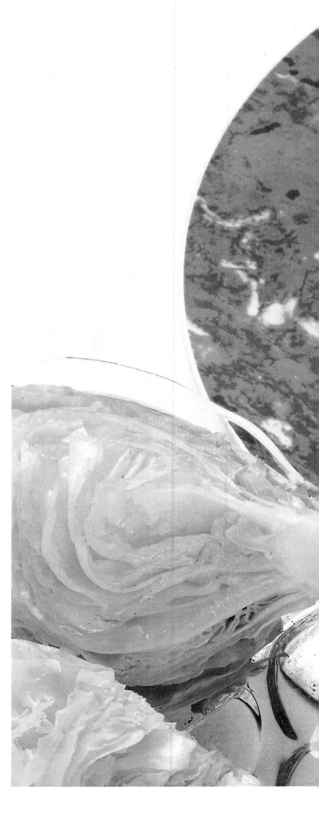

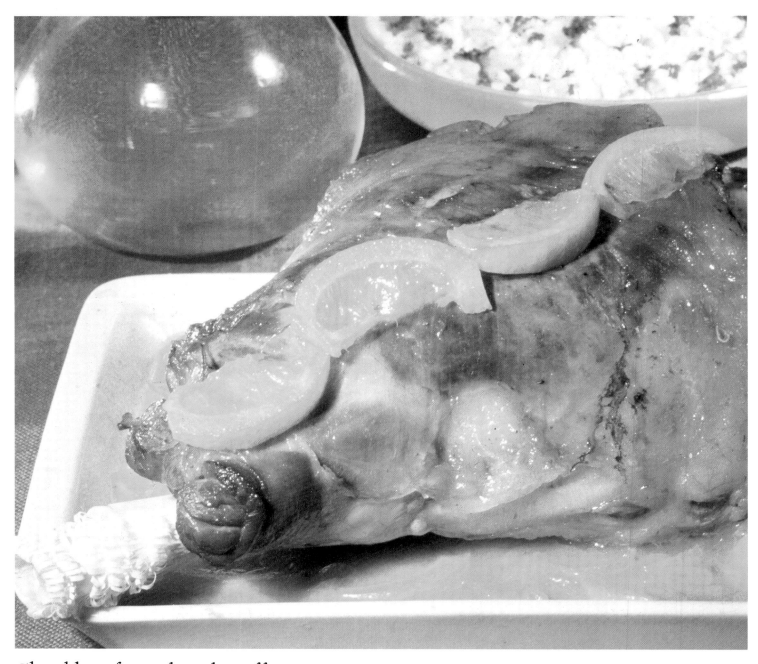

Shoulder of Lamb with Saffron

3 garlic cloves, peeled
2½ pounds shoulder of lamb
1 teaspoon Italian seasoning
salt and pepper
6 tablespoons olive oil
2 onions, sliced
juice of 2 lemons
pinch of cayenne pepper
saffron, to color

SERVES 4

Chop the garlic into slivers and insert it in small cuts all over the lamb. Mix together the herbs, salt and pepper and half the oil and marinate the lamb in this mixture for 2 hours.

In a deep, large skillet, sauté the onion in the remaining oil until golden brown, then add the juice of 1 lemon. Season with cayenne pepper and simmer for 5 minutes. Transfer to a large casserole. Preheat the oven to 350°F.

Heat the marinade oil in the skillet, then add the lamb and sear on all sides. Add the juice of the second lemon mixed with the saffron and transfer to the casserole. Cook until tender, 1½ to 2 hours.

Serve the lamb, carved into slices, garnished with sliced lemon and accompanied by rice.

Roast Leg of Lamb with Yogurt and Lemon

*1 shoulder or leg of lamb, about
 4 pounds*

*salt and freshly ground black
 pepper*

4 cloves garlic

6 tablespoons olive oil

*6 tablespoons lemon juice, plus
 a little grated lemon peel*

⅔ cup plain yogurt

SERVES 6 to 8

You can use either a shoulder or a leg – a shoulder serves fewer but the meat is sweeter when it is prepared this way. Season the lamb well with salt and black pepper. Cut the garlic into small slivers and insert in cuts all over the leg. Set aside for 4 hours. Meanwhile, preheat the oven to 450°F.

Heat the oil in a roasting pan in the oven until it sizzles, then sear the lamb on all sides which will take about 15 minutes. Remove the pan from the oven and leave the lamb to cool slightly, then pour half

the lemon juice, the peel and half the yogurt over. Reduce the oven temperature to about 375°F.

Return the lamb to the oven and roast for about 1½ hours, turning once and adding more lemon juice and yogurt. Add water if the lemon juice dries up. Do not turn after the final hour so the yogurt forms a golden brown crust. The total roasting time will be about 1¾ hours.

Serve this crusty tender lamb in slices, with boiled new potatoes sprinkled with cumin, and any of the green salads.

Okra and Lamb Stew

1 ½ pounds young okra pods
vinegar
3 cloves garlic, crushed
2 onions, chopped
1 teaspoon ground coriander
1 ½ tablespoons butter
2 pounds lean lamb, cubed
6 medium ripe tomatoes,
*   chopped*
1 ½ cups meat stock
salt and freshly ground black
*   pepper*
1 ½ tablespoons lemon juice

SERVES 4 to 5

Wash the okra and cut off the stems, taking care not to puncture the pods. Soak the pods in vinegar for 30 minutes, then drain them and dry on paper towels.

Sauté the garlic, onion and coriander in the butter in a large saucepan or flameproof casserole, then add the lamb and seal over a high heat. Turn each piece until it changes color, then add the okra and tomatoes. Simmer for 5 to 10 minutes, then cover with the stock. Season with salt and pepper, stir well, and simmer over low heat for 1½ to 2 hours, or until tender. By this time the sauce should be greatly reduced. Stir in the lemon juice just before serving.

Lamb and Chick-Pea Casserole

1 1/3 cups dried chick-peas
1 large onion, chopped
4 cloves garlic, finely chopped
1 teaspoon ground allspice
1 teaspoon paprika
pinch of ground coriander
salt and freshly ground black
　pepper
5 tablespoons olive oil
2 pounds boned lamb, cut into
　cubes
1 shin bone with marrow,
　chopped into 2 or 3 pieces
2 1/2 cups water
2 small eggplants
1 1/2 tablespoons lemon juice
6 tablespoons tahini (sesame
　seed paste)

SERVES 4

Soak the chick-peas overnight in cold water. The next day, drain them well and rinse.

Sauté the onion, garlic and seasonings in half the oil. Add the pieces of lamb and brown them quickly on all sides.

Place the meat and onion mixture, the marrow bones and water into a deep, heavy based flameproof casserole and simmer over low heat, stirring occasionally, until tender.

Remove the casserole from the heat and leave the mixture to cool. Take out the bones and extract the marrow, dropping it into the stew. Set the casserole aside while you prepare the eggplants.

Thinly slice the eggplants and lay the slices on a wooden board and sprinkle with salt. Leave for 1 hour, then rinse

under cold water and pat dry with paper towels.

Fry the eggplants in the remaining oil. Drain well on paper towels and keep warm.

Skim off any fat which has settled on the casserole, then add salt and pepper and stir in the lemon juice and *tahini* paste.

Stir well, then add the eggplant slices and keep the casserole in a warm oven until ready to serve. Serve with pita bread to mop up the rich sauce, and a well-seasoned potato salad.

Braised Chops with Vegetables

zucchini or leeks, see recipe

8 to 10 fleshy lamb chops

1½ tablespoons butter

1 large onion, sliced

2 to 3 cloves garlic, chopped

generous pinch of ground coriander, paprika and ground allspice

6 medium ripe tomatoes, sliced

2 tablespoons finely chopped parsley

salt and freshly ground black pepper

¾ cup stock

SERVES 4

Use 2 large zucchini or about 1 pound leeks. Preheat the oven to 375°F.

Trim the chops of any excess fat, then brown them in butter on both sides. Remove from the skillet and place in a greased baking dish.

Sauté the onion, garlic and spices in the butter remaining in the skillet until softened. Add the tomatoes, half the parsley and salt and pepper. Simmer for 10 minutes, then add the stock, stirring together thoroughly.

Place the sliced vegetables on top of the chops, then pour the sauce mixture over them. Add more seasoning, as desired.

Cook in the oven until the chops are tender and the sauce is rich and aromatic. Garnish with the remaining parsley.

Serve with mashed or baked potatoes, slashed open and topped with butter and ground cumin.

Meatballs in Yogurt Sauce

½ cup bulghur *(cracked wheat), soaked and dried*

2 pound lean ground beef

pinch of paprika and ground allspice

salt and freshly ground pepper

3 medium onions, very finely chopped

⅓ cup pine nuts

1½ tablespoons butter

cooking oil

Yogurt sauce

1 cup plain yogurt

1 tablespoon cornstarch

salt and pepper, to taste

2–3 cloves garlic, crushed

2 tablespoons dried mint, crushed

butter for frying

SERVES 4

Wash the *bulghur* and soak it in cold water for 2 hours. Squeeze dry in a clean dish towel. Mix together the meat, *bulghur* and spices, and mix to a pastelike consistency. Meanwhile, sauté the onions and pine nuts lightly in the butter, then set aside to cool.

Break off lumps of meat the size of a golf ball and stuff each with the pine nut and onion mixture. Heat the oil in a deep saucepan and fry the meatballs until crisp on the outside, but juicy within. Drain well on paper towels and keep warm.

To stabilize the yogurt, pour it into a large saucepan and beat until it becomes liquid. Mix the cornstarch with a little water to make a paste. Add this to the yogurt together with a pinch of salt. Heat to just below boiling, stirring continuously in one direction. Then continue to stir the mixture over low heat, or until the sauce

thickens. Do not cover or overheat.

Sauté the garlic in a little butter, then add the mint and mix this into the yogurt sauce. Season further according to taste. Place the meatballs in a serving dish and cover with the sauce.

Serve with plain rice and Arab salad, with pita bread to mop up the sauce.

Syrian Stuffed Kibbeh

½ cup bulghur *(cracked wheat)*
2 medium onions
1 pound ground beef
generous pinch of paprika
salt and freshly ground black pepper
cayenne pepper, to taste

Filling
1 medium onion, finely chopped
2 tablespoons pine nuts
about ¼ cup butter
½ pound finely ground lamb
½ teaspoon ground allspice
salt and freshly ground black pepper

SERVES 4

Make the *kibbeh* mixture first. Rinse the *bulghur* and soak it in cold water for 2 hours. Squeeze dry in a clean dish towel.

Grate the onion in a food processor, then add the meat and seasonings, and mix to a pastelike consistency.

To make the filling, sauté the onion and pine nuts in the butter. When they turn golden brown, add the meat and allspice to the pan, cooking lightly until the meat changes color. Add salt and pepper and mix well. While this cools, prepare the *kibbeh* shells.

Break off a lump the size of a small egg, and cupping in it in your palm, make a hole in the center with your finger. Mold the meat paste around your finger, working up and down and around and around (a practice likened by Claudia Roden, a Middle Eastern cooking expert, to pottery making). It is a difficult art: if the paste breaks, use moistened hands to stick it together again.

Now fill each egg-shaped *kibbeh* with a little stuffing. Seal the edges by wetting with iced water and pressing together. As each *kibbeh* is made, set it aside on a tray. (You can prepare them in advance and chill them.)

Heat a deep skillet with enough oil to cover the *kibbeh*. When the oil is sizzling, drop the *kibbeh* in and cook over high heat, turning frequently, until they turn rich brown but the filling remains juicy. Drain on paper towels and serve the kibbeh either hot or cold, with a selection of dips and salads.

The Syrians are masters at making kibbeh, *the pounding of the ground meat and* bulghur *being a familiar sound. Pictured here is stuffed* kibbeh *served with* hummus *(page 26) and* muhammara *(page 30) dips and pita bread.*

Ground Meat Kebabs

*2 pounds lean ground beef or
    lamb*

*3 medium onions, finely
    chopped*

*6 tablespoons coarsely chopped
    parsley*

*salt and freshly ground black
    pepper*

½ teaspoon ground allspice

½ teaspoon cayenne papper

flour for dusting

oil for brushing

SERVES 6

Light the barbecue (if using) or preheat the broiler. Put the meat and the remaining ingredients, except the flour and oil, into a food processor and work briefly until combined.

With moistened hands, break off walnut-sized lumps of the mixture and mold them into sausage shapes around a skewer (2 per skewer). You should fill 6 skewers in all. Dust with flour so they hold together firmly, then brush lightly with oil. Cook over the barbecue or under the broiler, turning frequently.

Serve on a platter lined with lettuce, garnished with lemon wedges.

Turkish-style Kebabs

2 pounds lean meat (see recipe)
salt and freshly ground black pepper
juice of 2 lemons
4 tablespoons olive oil
1 teaspoon chopped marjoran
paprika (optional)
1 red or green bell pepper
2 onions
2 firm tomatoes
4 kidneys, cored and trimmed (optional)

SERVES 4

Choose a lean piece of lamb or beef, then cut it into chunky cubes. Rub the cubes with salt and freshly ground black pepper and marinate them in lemon juice, olive oil and marjoram for about 2 hours. (To make the *kebabs* more piquant, add a good pinch of paprika to the marinade.)

Meanwhile, preheat the broiler. Cut up chunks of green or red bell pepper, onions and firm tomatoes to intersperse with the meat. Cored and halved kidneys are also delicious.

Spear the meat, onions, tomato and chunks of pepper alternately onto 8 skewers, then cook under the broiler, turning frequently until they are cooked on all sides. Serve 2 skewers per person.

Syrian Meatloaf

½ cup pine nuts

2 tablespoons butter, diced

2 egg yolks

2 medium onions, finely chopped

3 tablespoons tomato paste

1 teaspoon ground allspice

2 inch piece of fresh ginger root, grated

salt and freshly ground black pepper

2 pounds lean ground lamb

1 cup fresh bread crumbs

lemon wedges, and cress or parsley, to garnish

SERVES 6 to 8

First sauté the pine nuts lightly in a little of the butter and set aside. Preheat the oven to 375°F.

In a mixing bowl, beat the egg yolks, then add the onions, tomato paste, allspice, ginger and salt and pepper. Mix together well.

Knead the lamb thoroughly in a mixing bowl. Make a hollow in the center, pour in the egg mixture, add the pine nuts and mix well. Finally add the fresh bread crumbs to bind the mixture. Form into a loaf shape, and spinkle with a little cold water and dot with the remaining butter. Wrap in foil and bake for 1 to 1½ hours, unwrapping the foil for the final 30 minutes to let the top brown.

Syrian meatloaf may be served either hot or cold. This recipe leaves enough over to use cold; it is a good picnic dish. Serve with side dishes of *labneh* (page 28) and salad.

Kidneys in Tomato Sauce

12 lambs' kidneys
lemon juice or vinegar
2 onions, finely chopped
2 cloves garlic, crushed
pinch each of chili powder,
  ground coriander, ground
  cumin and chopped parsley
1½ tablespoons butter
4 medium tomatoes, skinned
  and pulped
1 tablespoon tomato paste
salt and freshly ground black
  pepper

SERVES 4

Soak the lambs' kidneys in water with 2 teaspoons of lemon juice or vinegar for about 2 hours.

Drain the kidneys, then skin, slice in half and remove the cores. Cut them into quarters.

Sauté the onion, garlic and seasonings in the butter. Add the kidneys and toss lightly until they change color. Add the tomato pulp and paste, stirring well. Add the salt and pepper and 1 to 2 tablespoons water.

Cook gently over low heat, 10 to 15 minutes, according to how well done you like kidneys. Serve with plain rice, pita bread and a green salad.

Pigeon is a great delicacy in the Middle East. Here a girl collects eggs in al-Fayyoum Oasis, near Cairo.

Poultry

One medieval Middle Eastern cookbook lists over 300 different ways of cooking poultry, especially chicken. Apparently Kaskari chickens (Kaskar is a village between the Tigris and the Euphrates) were considered to have the best taste and, according to one translator, they grew "as heavy as a goat, or a sheep." The breeding of chickens appears to have been common at this time, yet it was not so long ago, especially in the Arab countries, that chickens were so scarce that they were considered a luxury.

I recall an incident during my travels through Yemen when, invited to eat at a rural dwelling, I was sitting and talking to my host. A terrible squawking came from below, and peering out a window, I saw a boy chasing a scraggy hen until, with a well-aimed stick, he killed it. The fact that it was his father's only chicken underlined the family's incredible hospitality. Now, ironically, like most Middle Eastern towns, even the capital Sana'a has a KFC carry out.

It is probably true that there are more ways of cooking poultry than any other ingredient in the Middle Eastern repertoire. Recipes in this chapter range from chicken *kebab* to the exotic duck in walnut and pomegranate sauce. Finding we were only two one Christmas, I cooked Persian chicken (stuffed with apricots, prunes, raisins and pine nuts), which was as good as, and much more economical than, the traditional English turkey.

There is a delicious recipe for broiled lemon chicken (although it makes a mess of the broiler pan). I serve it hot with a green side salad, but it is equally good cold. I once made it my basic dish for a picnic to watch the Oxford and Cambridge boat race: it poured with rain and the Cambridge boat sank – but my lemon chicken dish saved the day!

The recipe for chicken casseroled with lemon juice was supplied by the Holiday Inn in Amman. Easy to prepare, it can be made in advance for a dinner party.

Ferakh al-hara (hot chicken) is one of the easiest dishes in the book, an ideal recipe should you be eating alone after a busy day at work. I have a very "seasoned" palate, liking things hot, and tend to substitute chili powder for the sweeter paprika.

Cafés in Amman, Jericho and Jersualem are known for chicken *musakhan*, a carry-out snack like *döner kebap*, or *shawarma* as it is known in Arabic. *Sumaka*, a red spice with a lemony tang, gives it the characteristic flavor, but this is difficult to buy in the United States.

As well as being masters at cooking chickens in so many different ways, Middle Eastern cooks take great pains to ensure that each dish has special eye appeal. Beautifully garnished with red paprika in oil and chopped walnuts, Circassian chicken is a good example. Side dishes are fluffy white rice and an emerald-green salad.

Fesanjan, or tender duck steeped in walnuts and pomegranates, is the king of all the poultry dishes. The medieval Persian recipe conjures up all the pomp and pageantry of the glorious reign of the Safavid *shahs*. If you can't find fresh pomegranates, use lemon juice or pomegranate juice concentrate, but the appearance of the dish will obviously suffer.

Restaurants in Lebanon have traditionally served small birds as *mezze*. Rubbed with salt, pepper and olive oil, they are grilled on skewers over a charcoal fire. A restaurant in the mountain town of Bhamdoun was famous for birds served in this manner. In Egypt, migrating quail are netted near Agami, a popular beach resort with Cairo's elite near Alexandria. Pigeons are kept by many families – elaborately built pigeon lofts are a feature in al-Fayyoum Oasis, near Cairo. Syrian farmers, especially around Aleppo, breed pigeons for the family pot.

Lemon Chicken Casserole

1 × 3-pound chicken, or 2
  small chickens
about 6 tablespoons lemon
  juice, plus extra for cooking
3 medium onions, chopped
3 cloves garlic, crushed
salt and pepper
pinch of paprika
1½ to 2 tablespoons butter
parsley, to garnish

SERVES 4 to 5

Skin and bone the chicken, then cut the
flesh into cubes.

Make a marinade of the lemon juice,
onions, garlic, salt and pepper, and
paprika. Add the chicken, stir well, cover,
and chill for 4 to 6 hours.

Remove the chicken from the marinade
and pat dry. Sauté the chicken in the butter
in a deep pan, adding 1½ cups water and
lemon juice to taste.

Cover and simmer over low heat until
tender, 30 to 40 minutes. Serve with
saffron rice (page 78), garnished with
extra paprika and parsley.

Chicken in Yogurt

6 tablespoons butter
2 medium onions, sliced
1 × 2½ to 3-pound chicken, cut
    into 8 pieces
pinch of salt
freshly ground black pepper
1½ cups chicken stock
6 tablespoons light cream
6 tablespoons plain yogurt
juice of 1 to 2 lemons

SERVES 4

Melt the butter in a skillet and sauté the onions until they are soft and translucent. Add the chicken and quickly brown on all sides, about 10 minutes over medium heat.

Add the seasonings and stock and simmer uncovered for about 30 minutes, turning occasionally. Meanwhile, preheat the oven to 375°F.

Mix together the cream, yogurt and lemon juice to taste.

Grease a casserole, transfer the chicken to it and pour the creamy sauce over. Roast about 1½ hours, or until the chicken is tender and the juices run clear if the flesh is pierced with the tip of a knife. Turn occasionally and add more lemon juice mixed with water if too much sauce evaporates. Serve with mashed potatoes, a green salad and bread for mopping up the rich, unctuous sauce.

Chicken Musakhan

*1 × 2-pound chicken, cut into
4 pieces*

2 cups chicken stock

1 small celery stick with leaves

1 medium onion, sliced

salt and pepper

*4 small onions, sliced into fine
rings*

1 tablespoon pine nuts

3 tablespoons oil

4 pita breads

2 teaspoons sumak, *if available*

SERVES 4

Place the chicken pieces in a flameproof casserole, cover with the stock and add the celery, the sliced onion and salt and pepper. Cover and simmer until tender, about 40 minutes. Remove the chicken and set aside a little of the stock. While the chicken is cooling, sauté the onion rings and pine nuts in the oil.

Arrange the bread on the broiler rack and top each piece with a portion of chicken, some of the onion rings and dribble a little stock over them. Sprinkle each with *sumak* and broil until the chicken turns golden brown. Take care not to burn the bread. Serve garnished with pine nuts and extra onion rings.

Musakhan can be eaten by itself, or with a salad. It is an excellent idea for lunch in the garden.

Circassian Chicken

1 × 3-pound chicken
1 large onion, chopped
1 clove garlic, chopped
2 celery sticks, chopped
salt and freshly ground black
    pepper
1¾ cups long-grain rice
½ cup walnuts, finely chopped
2 tablespoons olive oil
1 teaspoon paprika

SERVES 4 to 5

Put the chicken, onion, garlic, celery and salt and pepper in a large saucepan, cover with water and simmer until tender, about 1½ hours. Remove and drain the chicken, reserving the stock, then keep it warm in a low oven.

Chill the stock quickly, then skim off as much fat as possible from the surface.

Cook the rice (see page 78), and keep warm in the oven.

Meanwhile, make the sauce. Put the walnuts in a deep skillet with ¾ cup of the reserved cooking stock. Simmer, stirring until the mixture thickens. Season with salt and pepper.

Blend the oil and the paprika together until the oil becomes bright red. Cut the chicken into attractive serving portions and arrange them in a serving dish. Cover with the sauce and trickle the red oil over the top.

Ferakh al-hara Hot chicken

5 tablespoons olive oil
juice of 1 lemon
1 teaspoon chili powder, to taste
salt and pepper
1 heaped teaspoon crushed
  garlic
1×2-pound chicken, cut into 4
  pieces
lemon wedges, to garnish

SERVES 4

Preheat the oven to 375°F. Mix together the oil, lemon juice, chili powder, salt, pepper and garlic in a bowl.

Place the chicken pieces in a baking dish and cover with the mixture. Bake for 40 minutes, basting occasionally. Do not baste for the final 15 to 20 minutes so the chicken becomes crisp. Garnish with lemon wedges.

Serve the chicken with *pilav* rice (page 78) and a salad.

Persian Chicken

2 medium onions, finely
  chopped

½ cup butter

2 tablespoons raisins

1 cup dried prunes, soaked,
  pitted and sliced

1 cup dried apricots, soaked and
  sliced

1 teaspoon ground cinnamon

salt and freshly ground black
  pepper

1 × 3-pound chicken

SERVES 4

Sauté the onion in half the butter for a few minutes, then add the raisins, prunes and apricots and sauté gently for 5 minutes longer. Season the mixture with cinnamon, salt and pepper, and then leave to cool.

Preheat the oven to 375°F. Stuff the chicken with the fruit mixture. Sew up the neck flap to keep the moisture in. Rub all over with salt, pepper and then remaining butter, then wrap in foil and bake in the

oven for about 1½ hours. Open the foil after 40 minutes so the skin will brown and become crisp.

Roast Chicken Stuffed with Rice and Pine Nuts

1 large onion, finely chopped

½ cup butter, melted

3 ounces chicken livers, trimmed and ground

4 ounces sausage meat

½ cup long-grain rice

⅓ cup pine nuts

½ teaspoon ground cinnamon

¼ teaspoon ground allspice

salt and freshly ground black pepper

1 cup chicken stock

1 × 3-pound chicken

SERVES 4

Using a deep skillet, sauté the onion in two-thirds of the melted butter until it turns soft and golden. Add the liver and sausage meat and stir-fry until lightly brown. Add the rice, pine nuts, cinnamon, allspice and salt and pepper and cook about 5 minutes. Add the stock and cook over low heat until it is absorbed, 12 to 15 minutes. Leave to cool. Meanwhile, preheat the oven to 375°F.

Rub the entire chicken with salt and pepper. Spoon in the liver and sausage meat stuffing and close the openings with small skewers or thread.

Brush the chicken with the remaining melted butter and roast the chicken until it is crisp and tender, about 2 hours. To crisp the skin, do not baste for the final 30 minutes.

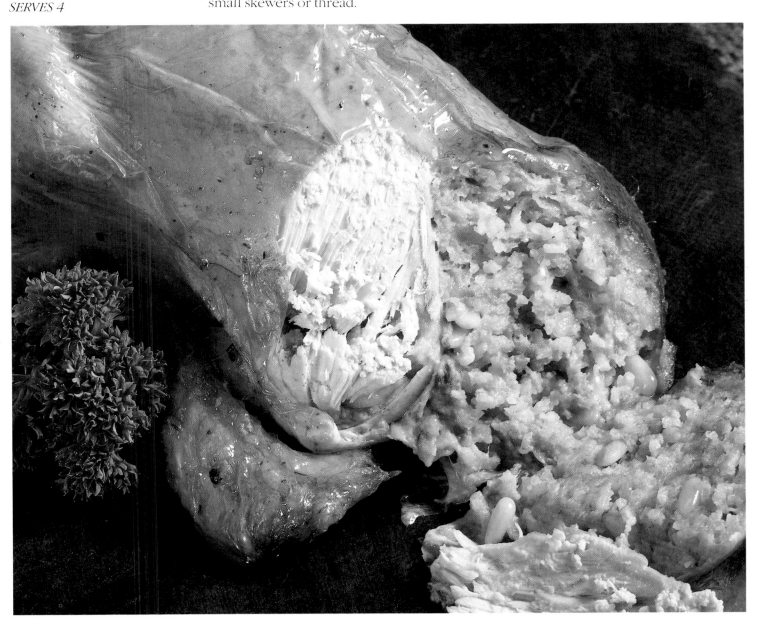

Chicken Kebabs

6 tablespoons olive oil

6 tablespoons lemon juice

2 cloves garlic, crushed

salt and freshly ground black pepper

1 × 2½-pound chicken, boned and cut into good-sized cubes (see recipe)

saffron or ½ teaspoon turmeric, to color

1 tablespoon butter, melted

SERVES 4

A barbecue is ideal for cooking these chicken *kebabs*, but a broiler is perfectly adequate. The chicken pieces should be of a size that will stay firmly on the skewers (leaving the skin on helps).

Combine the oil, lemon juice, garlic, and salt and pepper in a bowl, and place the chicken cubes in it. Cover and marinate for several hours, stirring occasionally. Preheat the broiler or light the barbecue.

Dissolve the saffron or turmeric in the melted butter. Thread the chicken pieces onto skewers and brush with this mixture. Cook over or under high heat, turning and basting frequently with the butter, for about 15 minutes.

Serve the *kebabs* on the skewers on a bed of Saffron rice (page 78), garnished with sliced oranges. A plain green salad complements the meal well.

Broiled Lemon Chicken

*1 large onion, very finely
   chopped*
juice of 2 large lemons
5 tablespoons peanut butter
¾ cup olive oil
salt, to taste
freshly ground black pepper
*2 × 2-pound chickens, each cut
   into 6 pieces*

SERVES 6

Preheat the broiler. Mix together the
onion, lemon juice, peanut butter, oil and
salt and pepper, then brush onto the
chicken pieces. Place the chicken pieces
under a medium-hot broiler and broil
until tender. Turn the pieces and baste
frequently with the mixture, watching so
that it does not burn. Serve the chickens
when they are golden brown and tender
and the juices are clear if the pieces are

pierced with the tip of a knife.
   The broiled chicken pieces may be
eaten hot, or cold, with a lettuce salad, rice
and pita bread.

Chicken with Olives

2 cups green olives, pitted and
    chopped

salt and pepper

3 cloves garlic, crushed

2 tablespoons olive oil

1 teaspoon grated fresh ginger
    root

2 to 3 strands of saffron

8 chicken pieces

1½ cups chicken stock

1 teaspoon paprika

1 teaspoon ground cumin

6 tablespoons lemon juice

SERVES 4

Bring the chopped olives to a boil 3 times in a deep saucepan. Change the water each time, the last time using 1¼ cups water with a pinch of salt. Remove from the stovetop and press the olives with a potato masher to extract more juices. Set aside.

Sauté the garlic in the oil in a large, deep skillet. Add the ginger, saffron, chicken pieces and the stock. Cover and cook slowly over medium heat, turning at intervals, for 30 to 40 minutes.

When the chicken is tender and the juices run clear, remove it from the pan and keep warm. Reduce the broth until

it becomes thick and pungent. Add the paprika, cumin, lemon juice and more salt and pepper according to taste. Simmer for 1 minute, then add the olives and their juices, stir well and leave the sauce to thicken more, 12 to 15 minutes.

When ready to serve, return the chicken pieces to the pan and heat through in the sauce. Serve each portion garnished with olives, with pita bread to mop up the sauce, *pilav* rice (page 78) and chopped salad.

Duck in Walnut and Pomegranate Sauce

2 medium onions, chopped

1 1/2 tablespoons clarified butter, melted

3/4 cup brown sugar

1 teaspoon ground cinnamon

9 tablespoons pomegranate juice (about 3 fruit), or use grenadine syrup

2 cups homemade stock

1 duck, about 4 pounds

salt and freshly ground black pepper

2/3 cup chopped walnuts

Garnish *(optional)*
2/3 cup chopped walnuts
seeds of 2 pomegranates

SERVES 4

Preheat the oven to 375°F. Sauté the onions in the melted butter until they are soft and transparent. Add the sugar, cinnamon, pomegranate juice and stock and stir well. Simmer over medium heat for about 10 minutes.

Rub the duck with salt and pepper. Increase the oven temperature to 400°F and roast the duck for 15 minutes. Remove from the oven and drain off any fat.

Spoon the pomegranate sauce over the duck, return to the oven at 350°F and continue roasting. Drain off the fat and turn and baste as necessary. Do not turn the duck for the final 1 hour of roasting.

When the duck is almost tender, add the chopped walnuts to the remaining sauce, adjust seasoning to taste, stir and simmer over low heat. Set aside and keep warm.

The options for serving are to present the duck whole, garnished with the rest of the sauce, chopped walnuts and pomegranate seeds, or to carve and pour the sauce over each portion. You can also put the remaining sauce in a gravy boat for people to help themselves. Serve with *pilav* rice (page 78) and a green salad.

The aroma of these freshly baked cookies wafts through a market in Manama, Bahrain.

Desserts and Confectioneries

The oldest-known Islamic confectionery is *faludhaj*, a Persian concoction of ground almonds, sugar, rose water and other ingredients, which is believed to have been introduced in Mecca to cater for pilgrims making the *haj*, or pilgrimage.

Ancient Arab and Farsi records make little reference to other rich desserts, but the Muslim sweet tooth can be traced back at least as far as the Abbasid caliphate. Recipe books from this period indicate that Abbasid society was addicted to confectionery, a taste not restricted to affluent families.

Among a variety of rich confectioneries were *lawzinia* (a confection of almonds, bread crumbs and syrup), *zalabiya* (an almond and rose water-flavored tart) and *khabis*, which seems to have been a gelatinlike dessert made with bread crumbs, milk, sugar and sesame seed oil. Sugar, honey, molasses and syrup were commonly used sweeteners. Many people in the Middle East still believe that eating honey and other sweet things will ward off the "evil eye."

Sweet desserts and confectioneries figure in many prominent dates in the Muslim calendar. Prior to *Muharram* (the first ten days of the New Year) or on the Prophet's birthday, housewives are busy baking traditional rich, sweet foods. It is a custom to take these to relatives and friends who similarly call with their own homemade specialties.

Baklava is probably the best-known dessert. I have eaten *baklava* in places as far apart as Dakar and Sydney – wherever there are Lebanese, Turkish or Armenian migrants. The Greeks also claim it is their own invention, but its true origins are obscure. *Baklava* is best eaten within a day or two of preparation. It can be made using either walnuts or pistachio nuts.

Basbousa is another syrupy dessert that can be made with yogurt or coconut. It may be eaten hot or cold, with or without cream. There is a horrible little store just outside Baalbek, in Jordan, that makes the very best *basbousa* in the Middle East.

There can be few people who have never tasted *lokum*, or Turkish Delight, as it is more commonly known. Many restaurants habitually offer a dish of it with coffee. I have not supplied a recipe for Turkish Delight as it can be readily bought and it is *so* time-consuming to prepare. Also served with coffee are delicate almond fingers, a truly magical confectionery that I have enjoyed in many Middle Eastern homes.

Ma'moul are bite-sized pastries of many different shapes and fillings. Outside the Great Ummayad Mosque in Damascus is a shop selling them oven-warm. You can buy a bag for less than two dollars to eat as you wander through the bazaar, one of the biggest and most interesting in the Middle East.

Dates have a myriad of uses in Middle Eastern cooking. The Bedouin often eat them with bread and yogurt as a substantial meal. They can be stuffed with marzipan or puréed to give a nutty flavor to fish. Tribes in remote parts of Saudi Arabia sustain their camels on date meal.

While the Palestinian town of Jericho is more famous for citrus fruit, bananas also flourish in the almost semitropical climate of the Jordan Valley trench. Plantations can be seen on either side of the River Jordan, and after the harvest, bananas hang side by side with oranges and grapefruit in Jericho's roadside stalls. Banana cake or banana loaf is an old Palestinian recipe, sometimes sold in stores, more often made at home.

Recipes appear here for three glorious Middle Eastern desserts. My own favourite, *ma'mounia* or "Caliph's Delight," is a recipe said to have been created for the Caliph Ma'moun. A specialty of the Syrian town of Aleppo, it is often eaten for breakfast, smothered in cream. Local folklore says it assists a woman to regain her strength after childbirth – what it does for men being something of a moot point. Similar to the drier *basbousa*, which is also made with semolina, *ma'mounia* is extravagantly rich.

Made from ground rice, *muhallabia* is to the Middle East what rice pudding is to the United States or England. A very simple, delicately flavored dish, it is eaten throughout the region; then under the name of *firni*, it pops up in Pakistan, having probably been introduced by the Mughal emperors.

Umm Ali, or "Mother of Ali," is a very rich dessert, very fattening and utterly irresistible if you have a sweet tooth. Dried fruit salad can be made with many different combinations of dried fruit and nuts. It is served when Muslims break the fast at dusk. Eat it with cream and be sure to make enough to have on your cereal – it's absolutely delicious.

"Caliph's Delight"

2 cups water

juice of 1 lemon

1 1/2 cups sugar

1/2 cup butter

2 tablespoons pine nuts,
    chopped

2/3 cup semolina

1 1/4 cups whipping cream,
    whipped

ground cinnamon, to sprinkle

SERVES 6

Combine the water, lemon juice and sugar in a saucepan. Bring to boil, then simmer for 15 minutes.

In a large skillet, melt the butter and lightly sauté the pine nuts. Add the semolina and cook over low heat until the semolina turns light brown, stirring, 5 minutes.

Remove from the heat and stir in the syrup. Return to low heat, stir well and cook for 5 minutes longer. Transfer the mixture to a serving dish. Smooth the whipped cream over the surface. Sprinkle with cinnamon and serve.

Umm Ali   "Mother of Ali"

10 ounces cooked puff pastry
1/3 cup shelled pistachio nuts,
    chopped
1/3 cup slivered almonds, toasted
1 1/2 teaspoons lemon juice
1 cup milk
3/4 cup sugar
a pinch of cinnamon
1 egg, beaten
2 teaspoons rose water
1 cup light cream

SERVES 6

Preheat the oven to 375°F.

Grease a round, glass baking dish, then crumble the pastry into the dish. Stir in the nuts and lemon juice.

Heat the milk, sugar and cinnamon to just below boiling point, then slowly add the beaten egg. Pour this over the pastry mixture in the dish and sprinkle with rose water. Top with the cream and bake for about 30 minutes until golden. Serve hot.

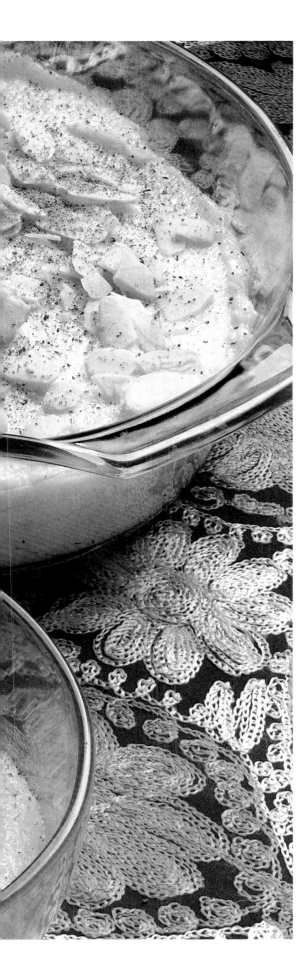

Muhallabia   Ground rice pudding

5 cups milk
3 tablespoons ground rice
1 tablespoon cornstarch
6 tablespoons sugar
1 tablespoon rose water
²/₃ cup blanched almonds, finely ground
slivered blanched almonds, or pistachio nuts, to garnish
grated nutmeg, to sprinkle

SERVES 6

With a little of the milk, mix the ground rice and cornstarch to a smooth paste.

Slowly heat the sugar in the rest of the milk, then add the rice paste, stirring continuously with a wooden spoon. Simmer the mixture until just below boiling point, and take care not to let it burn on the bottom because this will spoil the delicate flavor. The mixture should thicken in about 15 minutes.

Add the rose water and ground almonds and continue stirring in one direction over low heat. Simmer for 5 minutes longer, then remove the pan from the heat and cool slightly before pouring the mixture into an attractive glass serving bowl, or individual glass dishes.

Garnish with almonds or pistachio nuts, and sprinkle with nutmeg. Leave to chill for 3 to 4 hours before serving.

Banana Loaf

½ cup butter, softened
3½ tablespoons sugar
2 eggs
pinch of cinnamon
1 teaspoon vanilla extract
3 medium ripe bananas
¼ cup walnuts, coarsely
*   chopped*
1¼ cups all-purpose flour
2 teaspoons baking powder
1 teaspoon baking soda
pinch of salt
1 tablespoon milk

Preheat the oven to 350°F. Line a 9-inch bread pan with greased parchment paper.

Cream the butter and sugar together, then add the eggs, one at a time, beating well after each addition. Add the cinnamon and vanilla and beat together.

Mash the bananas to a pulp, then stir them into the mixture along with the walnuts. Combine well, then fold in the sifted dry ingredients, alternating with the milk. Pour the mixture into the prepared pan. Bake for 50 to 60 minutes, or until a skewer inserted into the middle comes out clean. Turn out onto a wire rack, peel off the lining paper and leave to cool.

Date Rolls

1 cup all-purpose flour
¾ cup plus 2 tablespoons unsalted butter, softened
1 tablespoon confectioners' sugar
1 tablespoon oil
1½ tablespoons milk confectioners' sugar for dusting

Filling
1½ tablespoons butter
1½ tablespoons water
2 cups pitted and chopped dates

MAKES ABOUT 24

Make the filling first. Melt the butter together with the water in a saucepan, then add the chopped dates. Cook over low heat, stirring the dates and pressing down until they become a soft paste. Remove from the heat and leave to cool.

To make the dough, sift the flour into a mixing bowl. Cut the soft butter into small pieces and work it into the flour with your fingers. Add the sugar and mix in thoroughly. Make a well in the center, pour in the oil and milk, then continue to knead the dough until pieces flake off the sides of the bowl. Knead for 10 minutes longer, then roll the dough into a ball, wrap in plastic wrap and chill.

Meanwhile, preheat the oven to 350°F. Grease a large baking sheet. Remove the dough from the refrigerator and divide into 3 portions. Knead each portion well.

On a floured board, roll out and flatten a ball of dough. Cut into a neat rectangle shape. Spread one-third of the date mixture thinly over the top. Roll the rectangle into a sausage shape and continue to roll backward and forward until it grows longer and thinner. Slice this into flattened circles about 1½ inch thick. Repeat this process using the remaining balls of dough.

Place all the date rolls side by side on the prepared baking sheet and prick the tops lightly with a fork. Bake for 25 to 30 minutes until slightly colored. (If you overcook them, they become hard.) Leave to cool, then dust with confectioners' sugar.

Baklava

*about 20 sheets phyllo pastry,
  thawed if frozen*
*1 cup unsalted butter, melted
  and clarified*
*1 1/3 cups chopped shelled
  pistachio nuts or walnuts*
1 teaspoon ground cinnamon
1/3 cup sugar

Syrup
2 cups plus 2 tablespoons sugar
1/2 cup water
1 tablespoon lemon juice
*1 tablespoon orange flower
  water*

Make the syrup first to give it time to chill. Dissolve all the ingredients together in a saucepan over medium heat. Remove the pan from the heat when the mixture thickens enough to coat a spoon, then cool and chill thoroughly. Meanwhile, preheat the oven to 350°F.

Grease a rectangular baking dish that is 12 × 8 inches. Lay 9 of the sheets of phyllo pastry in the dish, brushing the top of each with melted butter as it is laid down.

Mix together the nuts, cinnamon and sugar, then spread half over the top sheet of phyllo pastry dough. Place 2 more buttered sheets on top, and cover with the rest of the nut mixture. Layer up the remaining phyllo sheets, brushing each with butter as before. With a sharp knife, cut a diamond pattern in the top. Sprinkle with water to prevent the top layers of pastry from curling up during baking.

Bake for 30 minutes, then increase the oven temperature to 425°F. Bake for 10 to 15 minutes longer, until the pastry is puffy and the top is golden brown. If the top layer of pastry cooks too quickly, cover it with foil, but make sure that the pastry is cooked right through.

Take the *baklava* out of the oven and pour the very cold syrup over the hot pastry. Leave to cool. When the dish is completely cool, cut into small diamonds and serve.

Baklava, *the king of sweetmeats,
has Turkish origins (top right).*
Basbousa *(right) is one of many
Middle Eastern confectioneries
made with semolina.*

Basbousa with Coconut

¹/₂ cup butter
1 cup semolina
³/₄ cup sugar
¹/₂ cup shredded coconut
¹/₂ cup all-purpose flour
¹/₄ cup milk
1 teaspoon baking powder
vanilla extract
12 blanched almonds

Syrup
1 cup sugar
1 tablespoon lemon juice
¹/₂ cup water, boiling

First make the syrup by dissolving the sugar and lemon juice in the water. Simmer until the syrup boils and thickens, then remove it from the heat and set aside to cool. Chill. Meanwhile, preheat the oven to 375°F.

To make the "cake," melt the butter and mix it with all the other ingredients in a large bowl. Stir well, then spoon into a shallow baking tray.

Bake about 30 minutes, or until golden. Remove from the oven and cut into diamond shapes. Place an almond on each portion. Pour half the syrup over and bake for 5 minutes longer until the *basbousa* are golden brown. (Be careful not to scorch the almonds.)

Remove the *basbousa* from the baking tray and serve warm with remaining syrup poured over them. Although *basbousa* are usually eaten while they are still warm, they are equally good chilled, and will keep fresh for several days.

Ramadan Dessert

1 pound dried apricots
½ pound dried prunes
⅔ cup golden raisins
1 cup raisins
4 dried figs, chopped (optional)
2½ cups water
¼ cup sugar
*1 cup mixed nuts, such as pine
    nuts, walnuts and almonds,
    chopped*
light cream, to serve
grated nutmeg, to decorate

SERVES 6

Soak all the fruit overnight.

The next day, bring the water and sugar to a boil in a large saucepan. Stir 15 to 20 minutes, or until it becomes a syrupy consistency. Add all the fruits, mix together and simmer until they are soft but not breaking up. After 1 hour, add the nuts and stir well.

Remove the mixture from the heat and leave to cool, then chill. Serve in a cut-glass blowl or individual dishes. Pour light cream over the top and garnish with grated nutmeg.

Ramadan dessert is eaten when the Muslim fast is over at dusk.

Stuffed Dates

1 pound fresh dates, pitted

Almond paste
1 cup blanched almonds
1 large egg white
1½ cups confectioners' sugar
2 teaspoons almond extract
2 drops rose water
green food coloring (optional)

MAKES 1 POUND

Preheat the oven to 325°F. Spread out the almonds on a baking sheet and toast for 10 minutes, or until they are oily, but not brown. Set them aside to cool, then grind them in a food processor.

Add the egg white, sugar and almond extract, and process to make a firm paste. Add rose water, food coloring if using, and blend briefly. Chill overnight.

Open each date along the side where it has been pitted and press a small amount of paste into each. Cover and chill until ready to serve.

Almond Fingers

12 sheets phyllo pastry, thawed
½ cup unsalted butter, melted
¼ cup sugar
1¼ cups blanched almonds,
    finely ground
pinch of ground cinnamon
1 teaspoon rose water
confectioners' sugar

MAKES ABOUT 30

Slice each sheet of pastry dough into 3 pieces. Brush each sheet with the melted butter. While doing this, preheat the oven to 325°F.

Mix together the sugar, ground almonds, cinnamon and rose water, then spoon a portion along the middle of each phyllo sheet. Fold the sides in and roll up into a neat cigar shape.

Place the fingers in a row on a greased baking sheet and brush the tops with remaining butter. Bake for about 40 minutes until pale golden, then remove from the oven and leave to cool. Sprinkle with confectioners' sugar before serving.

Orange Slices with Cinnamon

3 oranges
ground cinnamon

SERVES 4

Choose navel oranges if possible. Peel and slice the oranges thinly, removing any pith and the seeds. Arrange the slices in a glass dish and sprinkle with ground cinnamon to taste. Chill, then remove from the refrigerator 10 minutes before serving.

Figs with Orange Juice

12 fresh figs
freshly squeezed juice of 6
*   oranges*

SERVES 4

This is a simple dessert which can be prepared in advance. Cut the stems off the fresh figs, but do not peel them. Quarter them and arrange in a flower design in a dish. Cover with orange juice and chill.

Date and Banana Dessert

1 pound fresh dates, pitted and
*   halved*
4 bananas
1 cup light cream
¼ cup roughly chopped walnuts
freshly grated nutmeg

SERVES 4

Fill either a glass bowl or individual glass dishes with alternate layers of halved dates and bananas. The dates should be as fresh as possible and should not be soft.

Cover with cream and chill for at least 2 hours so the dates absorb the cream.

Garnish with walnuts and freshly grated nutmeg, then serve.

These easy to prepare chilled desserts make an ideal end to a Middle Eastern meal: Figs with orange juice (top left); Orange slices with cinnamon (top right), and Date and banana dessert.

Hospitality is second nature in the Middle East. At the first sign of a visitor, coffee is put on the fire.

Drinks

Alcohol is forbidden by the *Quran*. This is not to say that several Middle Eastern countries do not produce some palatable wines: Turkey, Syria and Lebanon are wine producers and to a lesser extent, Egypt. The fiery aperitif *arak* is drunk in the Levant. The Turks drink it with the *mezze*, and, in fact, a *mezze* without *arak* (or *raki*) is unthinkable.

Muslim families commonly drink mineral water or soft drinks with their meals. Lebanon bottles mineral water, and the tiny Gulf emirate of Ajman supplies the whole of Arabia with fine mineral water that comes from an inland spring.

The ringing of the waterseller's bell is still a familiar sound throughout the Middle East, particularly in Egypt. The bearer of news, the waterseller has an important rank in street society. In the old days, other streetvendors used to sell fruit juices from glass flasks strapped to their backs; today, rows of juicers whizz in sidewalk cafés. Only in poor rural communities will you find someone still squeezing oranges by hand, or pressing sugar cane on a crude machine salvaged from automobile parts.

Fresh lemon, or better still fresh lime juice, is my favorite cool drink on a hot day. In 1964, after traveling across North Africa, I spent some time staying with my cousin who worked at the British Embassy in Cairo. Each afternoon, an old lime seller used to call at her flat in Zamalek, and on hearing his call from the street below, she would lower a basket for limes for our gin and tonics. And I particularly remember a tangy *limoonada* which revived me after a morning spent photographing the ruins of Persepolis, in Iran.

The ancient Persians were masters at making effervescent *sharbats* or sherbets from oranges, limes, apricots and other fruit. The pomegranate is a favorite fruit in Iran – it is said that the Prophet Muhammed urged his followers to eat it because it purged the system of envy and hatred. Using vivid metaphors, poets from Ferdowsi to the present day have compared the pomegranate to a woman's womb, ripe with progeny, to young maiden's cheeks, and the opened fruit to a broken heart, the seeds like tears of blood.

Tamarind juice is another popular beverage, especially in Syria and Iraq. The drink of nomads, yogurt and water, is commonly drunk with meals in Turkey and Yemen. Crushed almonds and milk is the stuff of the *Arabian Nights*.

Tea spiced with ginger and cinnamon is popular, but coffee, and the making and serving of coffee, has pride of place in Middle Eastern folklore; the whole coffee ritual is like a silent language that binds together both host and guest.

In traditional Bedouin society, a guest is invited to take his place by the fire in the men's section of the tent. The host then digs into the coffee bag and puts some beans in a ladle to roast in the embers. When they have cooled, he pounds them with a mortar and pestle, or *mihbash*, of traditional carved wood, or brass.

A skillful coffee grinder can pound out an appreciable rhythm audible at some distance, announcing to neighbors the arrival of a guest. The beans are tossed into boiling water, and after boiling several times the contents are poured into another pot and a pinch of freshly ground cardamom is added. This is allowed to simmer for about 15 minutes, the pleasant aroma pervading the whole tent.

The following gestures, now largely symbolic, remain essential protocol in the basic Bedouin coffee ceremony of the Middle East.

The first cup, offered to the host, is deemed the "unworthy cup," assuring the guest that the coffee is safe to drink and confirming to the host that it is hot, since it is a terrible insult to serve cold coffee. Like the other cups, the second cup is poured with the left hand, the bearer palming the tiny white china cups in his right. This second cup is offered to the guest, whose acceptance signifies he is pleased with the hospitality.

The third cup, even more significantly, has its roots in the days of tribal feuds. It silently concludes the protection agreement, meaning that the guest is safe from any attack while under the auspices of his host. This cup, known as the "sword cup," is binding, even against attack by one or the other's relatives. Sometimes a fourth cup of coffee is offered, confirming the silent defense pact.

It is not usual to drink more than this, but if a guest wants more (only a few drops are poured into each cup), he simply holds out his cup to be refilled by the attentive bearer. Alternatively, to signify he has had enough, he flicks the cup a couple of times with his wrist, the final concluding gesture to the coffee ritual.

Unfortunately, "Turkish coffee," as it is known in the West, is growing rare. High prices on the world coffee bean market have put many Middle Eastern coffee houses out of business, and in Mocha, the famous coffee port in Yemen, there is not even a drop of Nescafé! Chasing the quick profits from *qat*, local farmers have torn out their traditional coffee bushes and planted *Catha edulis* (*qat*) instead.

Qahwa (Arabic for coffee) uses coffee grounds and cardamom pods in varying quantities. It is served at every opportunity. You can be seated for only seconds in someone's home or office when, like a genie (or *djinn* in Arabic), a bearer arrives with a pot of *qahwa* and a stack of tiny cups.

On a royal tour of Saudi Arabia, as the only woman photographer, I often found myself *sans* men with the Queen in a harem. Emerging from a tent in Riyadh, about to step into her car, she was offered a cup of *qahwa*. Most of the time my presence was not acknowledged, but on this occasion her blue eyes glittered with humor: "This is my sixty-sixth cup of coffee since arriving in Arabia," she muttered, tossing it down like a Bedouin.

Yogurt Drink

3¾ cups plain yogurt
5½ cups iced water
1 tablespoon finely chopped
    fresh mint
pinch of salt
fresh mint leaves, to garnish

SERVES 4

Mix all the ingredients together, then pour into glasses, garnishing each with a little extra mint.

   Using sparkling mineral water rather than iced water makes an even more refreshing drink. Serve well chilled.

Yogurt drink (above left) is especially popular in Iran and Turkey, while Almond drink echoes the Arabian Nights.

Almond Drink

1 cup blanched almonds
sugar, to taste
1½ cups water
2½ cups milk
1 teaspoon orange-blossom
    water
few drops of almond extract
rose petals, to garnish

SERVES 4

Chop the almonds, then combine them in a blender or food processor with the sugar and water. Blend until smooth, then add the remaining ingredients. Garnish each glass with a rose petal.

Middle Eastern Lemonade

8 lemons
¾ cup sugar, or to taste
1 teaspoon orange-blossom
   water, or to taste
generous 2 tablespoons freshly
   chopped mint
still or sparkling water
ice cubes

SERVES 6

Squeeze the juice from the lemons and
sweeten to taste with sugar. Add the
orange-blossom water and the mint, and
stir or shake well together. Pour a little
into tall glasses and fill with water and ice.

Orange Sharbat

16 medium oranges
sugar, to taste
1 teaspoon orange-blossom
   water
water and ice cubes
sprigs of fresh mint, to garnish

SERVES 6

Pomegranate Drink

Squeeze the juice from the oranges and sweeten to taste with sugar. Add the orange-blossom water and mix together well. Serve diluted with ice cold water and garnished with mint.

2½ cups pomegranate juice
½ cup lemon juice
1 teaspoon orange-blossom water
sugar, to taste
sparkling or still mineral water

SERVES 4 to 6

Combine everything in a blender, or mix well in a pitcher, then serve with ice cubes.

Turkish coffee (left), Rose petal tea (center) and Qahwa are common hot beverages in the Middle East. Turkish coffee is drunk strong, while qahwa is rather bitter.

PAGES 148 AND 149 *A lavish and generous end to a Middle Eastern meal. Freshly made* Baklava *(page 132) and* Almond fingers *(page 137) are served with Turkish coffee, Turkish delight and fresh dates.*

Rose Petal Tea

rose petals from 4 roses
1 cup water
honey, to taste

SERVES 4

Choose fresh rose petals. Strip the flower gently under running water, then place the petals in a saucepan. Cover with the water and boil for 5 minutes, or until the petals become discolored. Strain into teacups and add honey to taste.

Qahwa Arab coffee

6 cardamom pods
¾ cup cold water
1 heaped tablespoon dark roast
    coffee, coarsely ground

SERVES 6

Bruise the cardamom pods by pounding gently in a mortar and pestle. Using a long-handled coffeepot (or a tiny saucepan), combine the water, pods and coffee. Bring to a boil, then simmer over low heat for 15 minutes until the grounds settle.

Serve *qahwa* in tiny white coffeecups – Arabic ones do not have handles – about 2 tablespoons in each. *Qahwa* is not served with sugar, and its rather bitter flavor is not to everyone's taste. It is, however, traditional Arabic coffee.

Turkish Coffee

2 tablespoons roasted ground
    coffee
1 heaped teaspoon sugar
3 small coffee cups water
tiny pinch of ground
    cardamom

SERVES 2

*There are three ways of ordering coffee in Arabic, and these are sweet (*helou *or* sukkar ziada*), medium (*mazbout*) or unsweetened (*murra*). Sugar is boiled with the coffee, and the quantity will depend on the preference of your guests. This recipe is for medium coffee, to give you an idea of the sugar quantities. If other guests require* helou *coffee, or no sugar at all, then you must brew another pot. Even if you like ordinary coffee without sugar, it is rare to drink Turkish coffee, as it is so sharp, without some sweetening.*

Combine all the ingredients in a long-handled coffeepot or tiny saucepan, stir well and bring to a boil. As the froth forms on top, remove the pot from the stove, stir again and return to the heat until the froth rises again. Be very careful the coffee does not boil over. Boil it briefly again, then set it aside for a few seconds.

Have the small cups ready to pour the coffee into, raising the pot (difficult with a saucepan) to get a nice head of froth on each cup. The grounds should be left to settle a minute or two before the coffee is drunk.

Index

A

Almond drink *143*
Almond fingers *137*
Arabian cuisine *12, 15*
Arab chopped salad *59*
Arab coffee *147*
Artichoke hearts in olive oil *33*
Asparagus salad *64*

B

Babagannouj – eggplant dip *25*
Baked eggplant with cumin *70*
Baked eggplants *69*
Baked fish with saffron rice *86*
Baked squash in tahini sauce *75*
Baklava 132
Banana and date dessert *138*
Banana loaf *130*
Barbecued fish with dates *87*
Basbousa with coconut *133*
Batata charp – stuffed potatoes *68*
Beid bi limoun – egg and lemon
   soup *48*
Beid ghanam – lambs' testicles *36*
Brains in lemon and olive oil *36*
Bread *6–7*

C

Cabbage rolls *71*
"Caliph's delight" *126*
Carrot soup *45*
Casseroles:
   Chick-pea and lamb *101*
   Green bean *72*
   Lemon chicken *112*
   Okra and lamb *100*
   Persian with prunes *95*
   Turkish vegetable *76*
Chelo – Persian steamed rice *78*
Chick-pea dip *26*
Chick-pea and lamb casserole *101*

Chicken:
   Broiled lemon chicken *121*
   Circassian chicken *115*
   Hot chicken *116*
   Kebabs 120
   Lemon chicken casserole *112*
   Musakhan chicken *114*
   Olives with chicken *122*
   Persian chicken *118*
   Roast, stuffed with rice and nuts *119*
   Wings with garlic and yogurt *39*
   Yogurt and chicken *113*
Chilled cucumber and yogurt soup *45*
Coconut with *basbousa 133*
Coffee:
   Turkish *147*
   Arab *147*
Cold fish in olive oil *82*
Cucumber and raisin salad with yogurt *60*
Curry (shrimp) *83*

D

Dates:
   Date and banana dessert *138*
   Dates with barbecued fish *87*
   Date Ma'amoul – date rolls *131*
   Date rolls *131*
   Stuffed dates *136*
Dietary laws *18*
Dolma – stuffed grape leaves *29*
Dried fruit salad *134*
Duck in walnut and pomegranate sauce *123*

E

Egg and lemon soup *48*
Eggplant:
   Baked *69*
   Baked with cumin *70*
   Dip *25*
   Salad *60*
Egyptian cuisine *12*
Etiquette *17*

F

Falafel – fava bean patties *30*
Fattouche – mixed vegetable and bread salad
   57
Fava bean patties *30*
Feast-day soup *51*
Ferakh al-hara – hot chicken *116*
Festivals *19*
Figs with orange juice *138*
Fish:
   Baked with saffron rice *86*
   Baked in *tahini* sauce *89*
   Barbecued with dates *87*
   Cold in olive oil *82*
   Fried *84*
   In hot sauce *88*
   Roe dip *26*
   Soup *49*
Fruit salad (dried) *134*

G

Grape leaves, stuffed *29*
Green bean stew *72*
Green bean, leek and asparagus salad *65*
Green pepper salad *62*

H

Herb and nut omelet *74*
Hot pepper dip – *muhammara 30*
Hummus – chick-pea dip *26*

I

Imam bayildi 69
Iraqi cuisine *16–17*

J

Jordanian cuisine *8, 11*

K

Kadin Budu – "Lady's thighs" *24*
Kebabs:
    Chicken *120*
    Ground meat *106*
    Turkish-style *107*
Kibbeh bi laban – meatballs *107*
Khoubz Arabieh – pita bread *41*
Kidney bean salad *57*
Kidneys in tomato sauce *109*

L

Labneh – thick yogurt *28*
"Lady's thighs" – *kadin budu 24*
Lamb:
    Braised chops and vegetables *102*
    and chick-pea casserole *101*
    Levantine stew *94*
    and okra stew *100*
    Roast leg with yogurt and lemon *99*
    Roast stuffed neck *96*
    Shoulder with saffron *98*
Lebanese cuisine, *8–11*
Lebanese "National" salad *32*
Leek salad *65*
Lemonade *144*
Lentil soup *51*
Levantine lamb stew *94*
Liver (fried) *36*

M

Meatballs in yogurt sauce *103*
Meatloaf (Syrian) *108*
Middle Eastern lemonade *144*
Muhallabia – ground rice pudding *129*
Muhammara – hot pepper dip *30*
Mussels (fried) *39*

N

Nut and herb omelet *74*

O

Okra and lamb stew *100*
Okra stew *73*
Orange juice with figs *138*
Orange *sharbat 144*
Orange slices with cinnamon *138*

P

Pepper dip (hot) *30*
Persian casserole with prunes *95*
Persian cuisine *16*
Pickled chili peppers *40*
Plain *pilau* rice *78*
Pomegranate drink *145*
Potato salad *62*
Potatoes (stuffed) *68*

Q

Qahwa – Arab coffee *147*

R

Raisin and cucumber salad with yogurt *60*
Ramadan dessert *134*
Rice:
    Ground rice pudding *129*
    Persian steamed rice – *chelo 78*
    Plain *pilau* rice *78*
    Saffron rice *78*
Roast stuffed neck of lamb *96*
Rose petal tea *147*

S

Saffron rice *78*
Salata Arabieh – Arab chopped salad *57*
Salata fil-fil – green pepper salad *62*
Samak al-hara – fish in hot sauce *48*
Sanbusak – stuffed crescent pastries *34, 35*
Sesame paste dip – *tahini 26*
Shoulder of lamb with saffron *98*
Shrimp curry *83*
Shrimp in tomato sauce *85*
Spices *19*

Spinach

Spinach pie *77*
Spinach salad *60*
Squash baked in *tahini* sauce *75*
Squid – stuffed *91*
Stuffed:
    Crescent pastries *34, 35*
    Grape leaves *29*
    Potatoes *68*
    Tomatoes *68*
Syrian cuisine *8–11*
Syrian meatloaf *108*
Syrian stuffed *kibbeh 105*

T

Tabbouleh – Lebanse "National" salad *32*
Tahini – sesame paste dip *26*
Tahini sauce with baked fish *89*
Tahini sauce with baked squash *75*
Taramasalata – fish roe dip *26*
Thick yogurt *28*
Tomato:
    and cilantro salad *62*
    sauce with kidneys *109*
    sauce with shrimp *85*
    soup *44*
    stuffed *68*
Tuna shashlik *90*
Turkish coffee *147*
Turkish cuisine *11–12*
Turkish-style *kebabs 107*
Turkish vegetable casserole *76*

U

Umm Ali – "Mother of Ali" *127*

V

Vegetable and bread salad *57*
Vegetable casserole *76*
Vegetable and beef soup *52*

Y

Yemeni cuisine *15–16*
Yogurt soup *45*

Z

Zucchini soup *53*
Zucchini with tomatoes *72*

Acknowledgments

I would like to thank the following for their assistance with this book: Gulf Air, the national airline of Bahrain, Qatar and the Sultanate of Oman, which features Middle Eastern delicacies on its in-flight menu; Hilton Hotels Middle East and the Sheraton Hotels in Cairo and Sana'a. The Mena House Oberoi and the Khan el-Kalili Restaurant in Cairo were also very helpful, as were dozens of other small restaurants and local cooks who provided background information on food and cooking.

Christine Osborne

PICTURE CREDITS
Theo Bergström 14, 22–3, 24, 26–7, 28–9, 32–3, 34–5, 36–7, 38–9, 40–1, 44, 46–7, 49, 50–1, 52–3, 56–7, 58–9, 60–1, 62–3, 64–5, 68–9, 72–3, 74–5, 76–7, 78–9, 82–3, 84, 87, 88–9, 94, 96–7, 99, 100, 102–3, 104–5, 106, 108–9, 112, 114–5, 116–7, 118–9, 121, 122–3, 126–7, 128–9, 130, 132–3 top, 134–5, 137, 138–9, 142–3, 144–5, 146–7, 148–9, front and back end papers

Michael Boys Syndication 15

Avi Ganor cover

Christine Osborne/Middle Eastern Pictures title page, 4, 6, 9, 10, 13, 17, 18, 20, 30–1, 42, 54, 64, 80, 92, 110, 124, 140, back cover

Paris Graphic 25, 48, 70–1, 90–1, 98, 101, 107, 113, 120, 131, 133 bottom, 136

Multimedia Books Limited have endeavoured to observe the legal requirements with respect to suppliers of photographic material.